Contents

Foreword by Neil Hawke 5
Introduction 7
1 India, at home, 1952 13
2 Australia, at home, and West Indies, on tour, 1953 24
3 South Africa, at home, 1955 and Australia, at home, 1956 41
4 West Indies, at home, 1957 50
5 New Zealand, at home, 1958 61
6 Australia and New Zealand, on tour, 1958–9 70
7 India, at home, 1959 84
8 West Indies, on tour, 1959–60 99
9 South Africa, at home, 1960 124
10 Australia, at home, 1961 140
11 Pakistan, at home, 1962 158
12 Australia and New Zealand, on tour, 1962–3 168
13 West Indies, at home, 1963 183
14 Australia, at home, 1964 195
15 New Zealand, at home, 1965 207
Index 219

I would like to thank, particularly, Peter Parfitt, whose advice when I first started to write this book proved invaluable: 'If you want to write a book about Fred, then do it and don't be put off by anybody.'

I am grateful to Neil Hawke who gave me a lot of help and encouragement, and also, of course, to Fred Trueman who made it all possible.

C. D. Clark

The Test Match Career of Freddie Trueman

C. D. Clark

DAVID & CHARLES
Newton Abbot London North Pomfret (Vt)

British Library Cataloguing in Publication Data

Clark, C D
The test match career of Freddie Trueman.
1. Trueman, Fred 2. Cricket – England – History – 20th century
I. Title
796.358'65'0924 GV915.T7

ISBN 0–7153–7944–5

Library of Congress Catalog Card Number

Photoset by Northampton Phototypesetters Ltd
and printed in Great Britain
by Biddles of Guildford
for David & Charles (Publishers) Limited
Brunel House Newton Abbot Devon

Published in the United States of America
by David & Charles Inc
North Pomfret Vermont 05053 USA

Foreword

There would have appeared to have been a never-ending stream of books written about Fred Trueman, but never before has somebody explored in such depth the sometimes turbulent pathway the Yorkshire bowler trod in achieving his own Everest by becoming the first bowler to reach 300 Test wickets. That I should have played a significant part in that milestone on a sunny day at the Oval in 1964 was a happy coincidence which created an immortality for me of a different kind.

Fred and I had, however, extended the hand of friendship some two years before when he toured Australia under Ted Dexter's leadership. What readily impressed me was his ability to communicate with the crowd without ever once losing his concentration for what was happening in the middle.

Seeing me alone at dinner in a top Sydney hotel he called me to his table for a night of excellent company and two unforgettable hour-long performances by the late Nat King Cole. I like to feel we have enjoyed a close friendship since and there have certainly been many social occasions and occasional cricket outings which would tend to substantiate this.

Even today, there is something majestic about that bowling action which makes one feel a little nostalgia for the days when Trueman electrified the atmosphere when claiming the new ball for England. Then his pride, matched by a heart which could not surrender, and fortified by a patriotic love for his country, made him an irrepressible tormentor of opposing batsmen.

Never, in my recall, did I ever see him raise the white flag—except in Adelaide one hot Foundation Day when the traditional twenty-six gun salute commenced at the nearby Torrens Parade Ground. It was beyond his nature to bowl to contain. Fred would trade blow for blow, probing, intimidating, watching, waiting for the chink in the armour to appear that would see the batsman on his way. Yet he was never short of appreciation for a fine stroke played against him, or praise for a great innings. Certainly he begrudged conceding runs from his bowling, but knew strokes were being played and the odds were swinging his way.

Chris Clark came to speak to me about his book on Fred's career, and such was his devotion to his hero that I had little doubt that it would be most well researched and most readable. For those who wish methodically and statistically to pursue the career of a very great fast bowler, it is an absolute gem.

In reading through each chapter, which traces the ups and downs of Fred Trueman's Test career, try and absorb the price he may have paid in terms of wickets and recognition for supposed indiscretions of youth. How many more times might he have played for England had he been less outspoken and perhaps a little less honest.

The character which was Fred Trueman then, remains the same today. Throughout the world he continues to entertain, but today it is the stories of yesterday which bring the audiences flocking in to relive some of his great and humorous moments of years gone by. Changes are occurring in cricket today which leave one with the impression that it may never be the same again.

Thank goodness future generations will have a most informative, well-written book on one of cricket's all time greats who had the ability to bowl his heart out yet radiate to all around a great sense of fun and enjoyment.

Neil Hawke
1979

Introduction

Superlatives abound in the world of sport. They are a necessary part of its overall picture, but unfortunately, one adjective in particular seems to recur with depressing regularity, namely, the word 'great'. Such is the frequency with which 'great' is employed by commentators and writers alike that it has assumed a multi-purpose use which covers almost every eventuality during any given sporting occasion. Consequently, anomalies are bound to occur. Events which border on the miraculous are often linked in the same breath or sentence with the more mundane efforts of mere man and only one conclusion can be drawn from this state of affairs. 'Great' is the most misused, over-used word in the sporting vocabulary.

All too easily does the word fall from the lips or spring from the pen. Of all the words available 'great' has transcended all others. 'X' made a great save; 'Y' scored a great try; 'Z' took a great catch. These word-pictures can be read every day of the week in various sporting publications, yet they mean nothing because with such liberal use of a single word the task of conveying a description of man's achievements in the sporting arena becomes over-simplified. If, in every instance, the accounts were true then great sportsmen adorn every corner of sport in their thousands whereas, in reality, the exact opposite is much nearer to the truth; greatness belongs to only a tiny fraction of the thousands who collectively comprise the whole spectrum of sport. As a result, the word 'great' is summarily banished from all of the following pages, with the exception of the very last page of this book.

When arriving at the name of the principal character about to be placed under the metaphorical microscope it will serve the purpose to draw an analogy with the mystical, heavenly world of astrology. Hopefully, this will place in a much more meaningful perspective one man's personal record in his chosen sport than would be the case with the glib use of simple, patronising five-letter words.

The sport in question is cricket, and, initially, any comparison between cricket and astrology would appear to be totally ludicrous. The stars and planets in the galaxies are far removed from the lush, green carpet tread by modern day disciples of W. G. Grace at such stadia as Lord's, the Oval, Old Trafford and many more around the world. Yet, paradoxically, the two do have some common ground. They both provide the watching world with one basic spectacle—phenomenon.

A simple illustration is the astrological sight known as Halley's

Comet. Only once every seventy-five years is the earth blessed with its presence, blazing a glorious multi-coloured trail across the skies before disappearing for another three-quarters of a century. A similar observation can be made about cricket, though thankfully not on quite the same time-scale. Nevertheless, batsmen or bowlers who truly set the game alight by their personality, expertise and sheer brilliance arrive on the Test Match stage all too rarely. Therefore, when they do, it is worth noting their exceptional talents and exploits with far more care than the deeds of lesser players.

Halley's Comet is a once-in-a-lifetime sight, not even that for many people, and the same applies to the really outstanding cricketers of any given era. A number of very good players appear briefly on the scene only to fade away without creating a lasting impression and, perhaps sadly, theirs must always be a case of 'what might have been'.

Conversely, and much less frequently, others come along to leave an indelible mark on the face of cricket and their names are justly etched into the annals of the game's history because of their accomplishments.

One such cricketer was Frederick Sewards Trueman, a fast bowler who found fame throughout the cricketing world. Fast bowlers come and go, but Trueman was one of cricket's rarities, a veritable gem among many well-gifted players. He had inestimable quality and inimitable style symbolising everything that was required to mould a man into the near-perfect fast bowling machine. Why near perfect? Simply because perfection can never be attained. It is the impossible dream but it can be made a goal always to strive for and, that being the case, Trueman came as near to becoming the perfect fast bowler as was humanly possible.

To be in the top rank among fast bowlers, supreme physical fitness, strength and stamina are essential and Trueman possessed all three in equal abundance. Without them it would have been impossible for him regularly to bowl upwards of 1,000 overs per season. Allied to these attributes, Trueman had the natural broad-shouldered, stocky build needed to sustain him through the rigours of his work.

By the end of his career Trueman had maintained his momentum over twenty years of first-class cricket with no more than a handful of minor injuries to prevent his playing the game for any lengthy period of time. That in itself, is testimony enough to the man's plentiful store of energy and willingness to expend it in the name of cricket.

Of course, the first-named ingredients are not the beginning and the end of a fast bowler's make-up. The most vital component has to be ability, not just in bowling but in the employment of all one's resources in the most beneficial manner. The first sign that Trueman had this added quality came with his bowling action. It was classical. There was a long, rhythmical run-up, whiplash delivery stride and explosive follow-through which catapulted the ball towards a batsman at a velocity in excess of ninety miles an hour. These were the hallmarks of an exceptional bowler but that was not the end. As well as the sheer speed was a masterful control of pace and Trueman was not averse to slipping in a fast off-break or the like to disconcerted batsmen. Once everything had been moulded into place and Trueman harnessed his speed with studious control, the near-perfect fast bowling machine was complete. Furthermore, a machine is a more than adequate description of Trueman in relation to his bowling because through twenty years of strenuous, back-breaking work he purred effortlessly like a well-tuned Rolls-Royce. Not coughing, spluttering and continually breaking down like a road-weary family saloon that was ready for the scrapyard.

Such a splendidly defined opinion comes not from the pen of the author but from Peter Parfitt (Middlesex and England) who played in the same England team as Trueman on numerous occasions between 1962 and 1965. Another with similar informed personal views to offer is Neil Hawke (South Australia and Australia) and together they give an interesting insight into the drama of a Test Match which is rarely seen by the average onlooker. Also, by virtue of being on opposing sides in their playing days, the comments of Parfitt and Hawke show a distinct contrast in the way various teams assess certain situations which arise during a tense Test Match struggle. In charting the course of the latter stages of Trueman's career (arguably the most important as that was when he claimed his major records) the contributions made by these two experienced former Test players are invaluable.

The heights of achievement scaled by Trueman far surpassed those of any other Test bowler prior to his arrival on the Test Match stage. Moreover, such is the standard set by Trueman that only a handful of players can be expected to overhaul him in the future but, as records stand only to be broken, it is natural to assume that a genuine fast bowler of his type will one day play Test cricket long enough to beat his record of 307 Test wickets. In fact, Trueman's world record was broken in 1976 by West Indian spin bowler Lance Gibbs. However, while Gibbs did claim the record, and without detracting from his glory, the circumstances leading up to the event were benevolent to the man, to state the case mildly. He was forty-one years of age when he finally clinched the record and, even for a slow bowler, that is an age which most veterans would begrudgingly acknowledge as being rather advanced for a Test cricketer.

On a different level, Australian all-rounder Neil Hawke gave a succinct précis of the situation by saying, 'There is little comparison to be drawn from the number of wickets taken by a slow bowler in relation to the number taken by a fast bowler. They are completely different and belong in two distinct, separate categories'.

When assessing the relative performances, Hawke's view is amply substantiated. Gibb's total number of Test wickets stands at 309, just two more than Trueman. Yet, to reach that figure, it took Gibbs not only twelve more Test appearances but some 12,000 extra deliveries than Trueman was allowed to play or bowl during his career.

On the question of age, it is an accepted fact that very few players are able to justify Test selection when reaching the age of forty and from that another salient point emerges. Once having wrested the record away from Trueman, Gibbs was never picked again to represent West Indies in a Test Match. The world record was virtually handed to Gibbs by the Caribbean selectors as a reward for long service. Notwithstanding these intricacies surrounding Gibb's final grasp on the world record there is, however, one indisputable fact. The record is his and his alone until somebody else takes it from him and all credit must go to Gibbs for having achieved the goal.

Trueman's Test Match career began in 1952. A long, hard, often rocky road lay ahead of him but somehow Trueman found the resilience to keep going despite the pitfalls, rebuffs and stinging criticism he continually had to contend with. In one respect, fortune did smile on him when he first exploded into Test cricket in 1952 with such instant success against India in that England did not possess a genuinely fast bowler of Test standard at that time. Along came Trueman to put the matter right in brilliant style but fortune's smile soon waned and his breathtaking performances against the Indians by no means guaranteed him a place in the national side; a place to which he was fully entitled and should have been his by right.

For whatever cause, Trueman found himself banished to the sidelines after eight appearances for his country. This exile was to last the better part of four years before the selectors had no other choice but to reinstate him in the team. In the light of future events, it was as well for England's cause that Trueman had the strength of character and unyielding will to succeed that enabled him to battle on when everything appeared to be set firmly against him until he returned to prove all of the critics to be so very wrong.

The following chapters trace this story of Trueman's progress along the Test Match highway which eventually brought him 307 wickets. It was a career spanning fourteen seasons, 1952–65, and embraces a total of sixty-seven appearances for England. Primarily, Trueman and his extraordinary bowling exploits are the main theme but there is also a parallel commentary on the cricket and cricketers of his era. At the time Trueman was carrying all before him there were many fine players around the world and it would be unfair to place him in a niche all alone. The other players deserve mention, not least for the part they played in aiding Trueman reach the previously undreamed-of figure of 300 Test wickets. Trueman predominates, but without the other players none of it would have been possible.

A simple chronological format is followed in the chapters ahead. From the start to the finish of his England career Trueman participated in nineteen separate Test series. By studying each one, every single appearance by Trueman in a Test Match can be covered, thus tracing the route of his 307 Test wickets from first to last.

It is the story of Fred Trueman's rise to sporting immortality and spans a career which encountered more than its fair share of turbulence. Primarily, only the exploits of the man in the field should concern the serious student of cricket but, unavoidably at times, events occurred of a decidedly delicate nature. In relation to Trueman's career, some of these were too important for them to be glossed over, therefore they must be dealt with as and when they arise.

However, a cricket writer is not a psycho-analyst and no attempt will be made to dissect Trueman's character. To have met the man is sufficient to prove the futility of the exercise. He is blunt, outspoken and down-to-earth, at times perhaps even coarse, but, above all else, he is very straight and honest and other than that no more needs to be said.

In his playing days Trueman had a goodly number of brushes with authority because of his extrovert playing style. He could be belligerent, noisy, bad-tempered and also extremely funny while on the field and these attributes to his game did not always meet with the approval of the MCC hierarchy. Therefore, some of his confrontations with the selectors were brought about by his own hand but, by the same token, it is abundantly clear that he was made to shoulder the blame for much of which he had no part whatsoever, simply because he was Fred Trueman. Much was written (and spoken too, behind his back) that should have been too asinine to bear the slightest consideration but once the label was attached it stuck to him throughout his entire career.

At the end of the day, when Trueman's long run-up was completed, there was only one simple fact to be remembered: a cricketer stands or falls by his own deeds on the field of play. Consequently, nobody can deny that Trueman accomplished what no other bowler, either fast or slow, had ever accomplished before. Whatever 'incidents' or 'affairs' may or may not have taken place during his career, or however galling they were to him at the time, Trueman was big enough and good enough to withstand them all and still come out on top. That was the perfect answer to each and every one of his critics.

1 India, at home, 1952

The summer of 1952 heralded the beginning of a new era for English cricket, an era dominated by Freddie Trueman who was to captivate audiences and torment batsmen from every Test-playing country for the following fourteen seasons. The first team to suffer at the hands of this new fast bowling prodigy would be India, embarking on their fourth visit to England since tours were initiated in 1932. The Indians arrived with scant prior knowledge of the terrifying barrage of fast bowling about to be launched at them by Trueman. He had yet to appear in Test Match cricket but the signs were already evident that it would not be long before he would be given his chance by the England selectors.

In April 1952, with the Indians barely arrived in England for the four-match series, *The Times* previewed the forthcoming rubber in an attempt to assess the home team's chances. In fact, the article was more concerned about the following season's visitors, Australia, than it was with India who were not generally regarded as being the sternest of opposition in world cricket at that time. Australia most certainly were and the cause for concern among contemporary commentators was the apparent lack of genuine pace bowling in the early 1950s to counteract the twin menace Miller and Lindwall would provide when they toured England in 1953. The prior series against India would give selectors and players alike the opportunity to put their ideas to the test in an attempt to find an effective answer to Australia's challenge.

By the end of the summer the picture had changed quite dramatically. In five short months the pessimists were eating their words and everybody had no doubt that England had found another fast bowler to follow in the footsteps of the giants of yesteryear. Trueman showed an extraordinary pace and literally smashed his way on to the Test Match scene against the Indians. Such were the devastating effects produced by Trueman, it was more like a volcano erupting than a fledgling fast bowler trying to make his way in the rough, tough world of Test cricket.

When the Indians returned home after losing the series three-nil with one game drawn they had been completely annihilated by Trueman. He had mesmerised, demoralised and terrified the tourists by the sheer speed and brute force he hurled their way via a cricket ball. It was true that the Indians of 1952 could hardly be called world class but when a young fast bowler makes such a shattering impact on Test cricket, as Trueman did in his very first series, it could mean only one thing. Here was no ordinary bowler but one with great potential indeed and the claim was entirely justified as Trueman went on to take that potential into full maturity over the next fourteen years at the highest level of the game. In doing so, he was to demonstrate a talent such as had never been seen before.

With benign respect *The Times* had noted Trueman as 'a promising young fast bowler'. This was an important appraisal; it signified Trueman's arrival as a Test Match candidate and his career duly commenced at Headingley, on 5 June 1952 in the First Test of the series against India. It is difficult to imagine a more appropriate place for a Yorkshireman to make his debut in international cricket and the long run-up had begun, not just in his bowling but in the length of time he was to remain an England player albeit intermittently in the early stages.

Result-wise, the game went England's way by a comfortable seven wickets, Trueman marking a highly satisfactory first appearance with a comparable number of wickets to his credit. In the tourists' first innings, nothing particularly spectacular was seen from the new recruit with the exception, perhaps, of the following scorebook entry:

P. Umrigar c Evans b Trueman 8

There, with a wicket to his credit for the very first time, was etched the name batsmen the world over would come to fear and respect. In the final analysis of this first tilt at the Indians, Trueman had figures of 26–8–89–3. It was a modest start but a start nonetheless along a road that would eventually take him further than any other fast bowler in the history of the game.

It was in the second innings of the game that the latent talent really sprang into being. The Indians plunged headlong into trouble and in less time than they would care to remember were in the unique position of having lost four wickets without a run on the scoreboard to show for their efforts. Never before had such a disastrous start been made by a Test team and for Hazare, the visitors' captain, the position bore another added significance. Not only had he the incredible scoreline to occupy his thoughts but he was also going in at number six facing a possible hat-trick. The previous worst start to a Test innings had been made some eighteen months earlier when England played Australia at Brisbane. It was the First Test of the tour and then Australia had crashed to nought for three wickets in their second innings. Wrote A. G. Moyes, in his account of the Test, 'The board presented a curious sight, one which we may never see again,' but now Trueman, with the aid of Bedser, had relieved the Australians of their dubious distinction. Trueman had taken three of the wickets to fall and was also the bowler on the coveted hat-trick. It was little wonder, therefore, that the exultant Yorkshire crowd roared its approval of their new hero on that third day's play. Mantri had been the first victim, clean bowled, followed by Manjrekar in exactly similar fashion but the ultimate glory was to elude Trueman. The third ball missed Hazare's off-stump by the proverbial coat of paint and the Indian skipper survived to bat on in a face-saving sixth wicket stand of 105, after the fifth wicket fell at 26. In fact, Trueman was never destined to accomplish the Test Match hat-trick even though, in the course of his career, he faced the prospect a tantalising six times. As for the First Test against India, Trueman went on to take just one more wicket in the second innings but he had stamped his mark on the game from the very outset of his career. The dye had been cast and the message for the rest of the summer was patently obvious. Indians beware!

History would have us believe that the Indians were terrified of fast bowling but this is a rather cruel indictment. There were numerous failures to stand up to Trueman's speed but there were exceptions to this. Vijay Manjrekar provides a perfect example. Then only twenty years of age he scored a glorious 133 in the tourists' first innings at Headingley out of a total of 293. It showed amply that not all the Indians quaked in their boots at the mere sight of Trueman and with Hazare, the young student set a record fourth-wicket partnership of 222. He was the exception to the rule, however, and the only other batsman to make a mark was Vinoo Mankad. His performance in the Second Test at Lord's placed him in the top rank of the world's great all-rounders but these two players were the only batsmen to show any real composure against Trueman.

Somewhat harshly, the Indians were branded as cowardly in the face of Trueman's onslaught in that they continually backed away from the crease when the ball was delivered. Some people even went so far as to say the batsmen actually ran away from the crease! Yet, when considering what they had to stand up against this was hardly surprising. The conditions the Indians were playing under were far removed from what they were accustomed to in their own country. The moist, green pitches and damp atmosphere made the ball move both off the wicket and through the air far more than they had previously seen. As if that was not disconcerting enough they then had to face Trueman. At that stage of his career he was undoubtedly the fastest, and often wildest bowler they had ever had the misfortune to encounter.

Under such circumstances the bemused Indians could hardly be faulted for taking evasive action. This was not cowardice on their part. It was a predetermined train of thought which sought to avoid injury at all costs. Not that this suggests in any way that Trueman deliberately bowled at the batsmen. Far from it, but once the Indians had conditioned themselves to taking such a course of action, nothing in the world would alter their frame of mind. The plain fact is that Test cricketers are not cowards and do not become so disposed overnight.

The Indians had seasoned campaigners among them but it was a lack of technique added to peculiar set of circumstances and events which brought about their seemingly untoward demeanour at the crease. From the way Trueman was seen to perform in the summer of 1952 it is doubtful if more than a handful of batsmen throughout the world could have faced him and honestly stated that some form of fear or trepidation would not pass through their minds. To be anxious, possibly a little frightened, is one thing (and no batsman should be ashamed to admit experiencing such emotions) but it is no concept for cowardice and such a description is an insult to the sporting integrity of the Indian tourists of 1952.

The series progressed to the Second Test at Lord's where England gained another comfortable victory. This time it was by eight wickets and once again Trueman's personal quota of wickets for the match corresponded exactly with the winning margin. His analyses of 4 for 72 and 4 for 110 were more than reasonable but they did show that accuracy was not yet one of his strongest points. Time and ever-increasing maturity would be needed before those facets were instilled into his play and it was crystal clear they would not be long in merging with the tremendous speed already evident.

The match was a comfortable enough stroll for England but it was also a personal triumph for the Indian all-rounder Vinoo Mankad, both in performance and endurance. When India batted first he scored a splendid 72 and followed it by bowling a marathon 73 overs during England's first innings in which they amassed 537 runs. This was not all. Mankad promptly opened India's second innings and scored a brilliant 184 out of a total of 378 all out. This was a truly remarkable performance and justified his high-ranking position among the world's leading all-rounders of the day.

England were now two-nil ahead in the series. It was clear immediately after the initial blast the Indians had encountered at Headingley that they would always be ill-at-ease against Trueman, apart from the odd one-man performances previously described and this was borne out in the Third Test when the bewildered tourists were humiliated in a way never witnessed before in a Test Match. In short, they met up with Trueman at his very best. So stunning was his performance it moved *The Times* correspondent to elucidate his opinion of the bowler in far more glowing terms than had been the case before the series began. After the rout of the Indians had been completed the correspondent wrote thus of Trueman: he had witnessed 'a piece of genuine fast bowling as spectacular as anything shown by an Englishman since the days of Larwood'. High praise indeed for a young man, who three months earlier had been no more than a promising prospect.

The Test was played at Old Trafford and solely in terms of figures England were the winners before close of play on the third day by the massive margin of an innings and 207 runs. But it was more than that. The game produced stupendous record-breaking events and provided Trueman with the best Test analysis of his entire Test career. It was his finest hour in a summer full of memories yet figures alone fail to do Trueman proper justice, impressive reading though they make: 8.4–2–31–8. For a one-innings one-man demolition job by a fast bowler those figures have yet to be surpassed in Test cricket.

It was not until the third day that Trueman began his march into the history books. This was to be a two-fold entry because, in addition to Trueman's own amazing feat, the occasion was the first modern instance of a Test team being dismissed twice in a single day's play. Exceptional as the figures were it was the manner and under what circumstances they were brought to pass which makes them really outstanding. The weather in Manchester on the third day was extremely poor. Dreary, damp, windy conditions were hardly conducive to fast bowling. Trueman cast these disruptive elements aside and bowling down-wind at his fastest produced the most exhilarating piece of fast bowling seen for years.

To a certain extent, Trueman was aided by some wonderful close wicket-catching. Again, this was rather remarkable under such cold conditions but it all adds to the splendour of the performance and the field set for Trueman cannot have been employed many times in a Test Match, either before or after that July day in 1952. Three slips, three gulleys, two short legs and one short mid-off meant every England fielder, with the exception of wicket-keeper Evans and Trueman himself, was clustered within yards of the Indian batsmen. What an awe-some sight that must have been for them! The full scorecard for the Indians' second innings read as follows:

ENGLAND *v* INDIA: THIRD TEST MATCH AT OLD TRAFFORD 17, 18, 19, 21, 22 JULY 1952

INDIA: 1ST INNINGS

V. Mankad	c Lock	b Bedser	4
P. Roy	c Hutton	b Trueman	0
H. R. Adhikari	c Graveney	b Trueman	0
V. S. Hazare		b Bedser	16
P. R. Umrigar		b Trueman	4
D. G. Phadkar	c Sheppard	b Trueman	0
V. L. Manjrekar	c Ikin	b Trueman	22
R. V. Divecha		b Trueman	4
G. S. Ramchand	c Graveney	b Trueman	2
P. Sen	c Lock	b Trueman	4
Ghulam Ahmed	not out		1
	Extras	lb 1	1
			58

FALL OF WICKETS

1	*2*	*3*	*4*	*5*	*6*	*7*	*8*	*9*
4	4	5	17	17	45	51	53	53

BOWLING	*O*	*M*	*R*	*W*
Trueman	8.4	2	31	8
Bedser	11	4	19	2
Laker	2	0	7	0

It was sheer speed which destroyed the Indians, but with it went a masterful control that gave firm evidence of Trueman's growing maturity as a fast bowler. The critics were not slow to lavish praise on this great new hope of English cricket. Here at last, they said, was a fast bowler to follow in the steps of Larwood. Why the comparison had to be made with Larwood is difficult to understand. That he had been a very good fast bowler there is no question but there the similarity ends. Larwood was never given the chance to fulfil expectations for England because he was cast aside as soon as the controversial 'bodyline' tour of 1932–3 to Australia had ended. Now, some twenty years later, Trueman had arrived on the scene but he could not be accepted in his own right. It had to be at the expense of meaningless comparisons with players of decades ago and not on the strength of his own meritorious performances.

Trueman's spell of bowling against India was not merely the best since the days of Larwood, it was the best in the whole history of the game. Trueman himself was never to better that performance at any time in his career yet the point can be made that other performances later in his career could be classed as more noteworthy. By no stretch of the imagination is this to detract one iota from Trueman's feat in 1952. A return of 8 for 31 by a fast bowler in a Test Match is magnificent world-class bowling by any standards but the point at issue is the fact that the analysis came in the course of one innings.

In 1961, against the Australians at Headingley, Trueman finished with match figures of 11 for 88, taking five wickets in the first innings and six in the second. Two years later against West Indies he performed with similar success but this time to such an extent that he took the amazing total of twenty-three wickets in two consecutive Tests. There is consistency of the highest degree. In the Second Test of the 1963 series Trueman's match figures were 11 for 152 while in the Third Test he took 12 for 119. This latter game was all the more remarkable when in West Indies' second innings Trueman blasted the opposition to oblivion with an incredible finishing burst which saw him take the last six wickets for four runs!

At once, when confronted with facts and figures such as these, problems arise for the statistician. Taking into account the comparative strengths and weaknesses of the various sides against whom these deeds were wrought, it is no easy task to evaluate the different performances and place them categorically one above the other. To use a simple analogy, is 5 for 60 on a plumb batting wicket better than 5 for 20 on a pitch ideally suited to fast bowling? People would have convincing arguments for both cases and the only reasonable solution to the problem is to take each match on its individual merits. Accordingly, Trueman's 8 for 31 against the Indians was his finest-ever, never-to-be repeated, single innings performance for England. On the other side of the coin, future Test Matches would see him produce superior sustained efforts over the course of both innings of a game and therein lies the difference in equating the respective merits of singular feats of achievement.

As for the Third Test in 1952, Trueman had little opportunity to carry on his rampage through the Indian batsmen. The second innings followed much the same pattern as the first but, by this time, the slower bowlers were in operation rapidly concluding the game and Trueman claimed only one more wicket to add to his first eight. It gave him match figures of 9 for 40 and he had played his part brilliantly with the initial bombardment which set England well on the way to victory.

England now had an unbeatable three-nil lead in the series. The Fourth and final Test at the Oval provided the home team with the rare opportunity of making a clean sweep of the series but the only winner was the weather. England's chance would come again in the not-too-distant future when the unfortunate Indians would again be in opposition, in 1959, but until then they would have to be content with a draw at the Oval. Over the full five days only ten-and-a-half hours' play were possible, ruling out the possibility of a definite result almost from the outset.

Not that Trueman had quite finished with the hapless Indians yet. In the few hours' play that were possible he tore through their batting for the final time in 1952. It was Trueman's last chance to plunder wickets and at one stage India were reeling at 5 runs for 6 wickets and he went on to take 5 for 48 from 16 overs. Mercifully for the tourists the weather intervened and their torment at the hands of Trueman was over. At the end of a wretched season they could turn their thoughts to the journey home after an unrelenting battering from England's newest recruit to the fast bowling fraternity. For Trueman, a final touch of success came in the Oval Test when he held his first catch for England in India's first innings. As with his bowling, it proved to be the first of many he would take throughout his career.

Thus, in his first Test series, Trueman had made an immense impact on the game. He did not take less than five wickets in any of the four Tests in which he played and altogether captured a total of twenty-nine wickets costing just 13.31 runs each. As could be expected, with such a high number of wickets to his name Trueman was easily the leading wicket-taker in the series. This was the first of nine occasions he would attain such a record for England in the nineteen separate series in which he took part during his career.

After such an impressive start to his Test Match career it would be logical to envisage Trueman being an integral part of England's team for years to come. Incredibly, it was to be five years before he would participate in a full Test series again in England. After the India series Trueman represented England in just seven more Tests in the interim period leading up to the summer of 1957. It was only then, when West Indies were the visitors, that Trueman finally managed to claw his way back into the national side on a permanent basis.

The reasons for Trueman's expulsion from Test cricket were many, varied and complex. As yet, at the end of 1952, there was nothing to foretell of the bombshells that would be exploded in the near future and Trueman was on top of the world. In no uncertain manner he had demonstrated a talent far superior to anything seen in an English fast bowler for years. The fact did not go by unnoticed and two accolades were deservedly awarded to him. First came the Cricket Writers Trophy for the best young cricketer of the year and when the 1953 edition of *Wisden* was published Trueman was among its five cricketers of the year for 1952. The rebuffs and criticism would start soon enough but until then Trueman could reflect in his new-found glory after a most memorable summer.

The next Test series would be for the Ashes the following summer against Australia and it was unfortunate in many ways that *MCC* had no official tour planned for the winter of 1952–3. Who knows how differently Trueman would have developed had he been able to embark on a foreign tour straight after his summer triumphs? Instead, Trueman would have to wait a full year before making his first overseas trip. That trip to West Indies was to cause incalculable harm to his career and in the meantime there would only be one more appearance in England before embarking for the Caribbean.

AVERAGES FOR 1952 SERIES *v* INDIA: Four Tests, Played Four

Overs	*Mdns*	*Runs*	*Wkts*	*Ave*
119.4	25	386	29	13.31

Inns	*NO*	*Runs*	*HS*	*Ave*
2	1	17	17	17.00

Catches=1

Match results=England 3, India 0, 1 Match drawn.

Statistics
1 Running total of Test wickets=29
2 Total catches=1
3 Total runs=17
4 Total appearances=4

N.B. Leading English wicket-taker for the first time.

2 Australia, at home, and West Indies, on tour, 1953

While 1953 did not provide Trueman with the same spectacular success as the previous year the one Test in which he played was sufficient to provide him with one of the happiest moments of his career. The opposition came in the form of Australia but it was not until the Fifth Test that the selectors deemed Trueman's presence necessary to the England team. Unquestionably, the Australians were a much sterner proposition to a bowler than the 1952 Indians had proved and Trueman was still serving his national service at the time, which could have prevented him from playing. Yet, similar circumstances had prevailed in 1952 when the selectors had little difficulty obtaining his release and it appears to have been deliberate policy to omit Trueman from the side, probably on the grounds of inexperience.

Experience can only be gained by playing. Trueman had advanced in age by a year and with the benefit of his four Tests against India behind him there was no reason to suppose he had failed to make at least some measure of improvement. Perhaps it was expecting too much for Trueman to have played in all five Tests in 1953. He was still very much a novice but, if not every game, two or three Tests would have been a fairer trial against a strong Australian team.

The call to duty was not made. Trueman languished on the sidelines throughout the season while England drew four successive Tests. The series and the destination of the coveted Ashes hung in the balance, depending upon the final game. Another draw was unlikely as the match was scheduled to run for six days instead of the more normal five and it was to this match that Trueman reappeared on the scene. Saturday 16 August was the appointed date for battle to commence at the Oval and Trueman duly took his place on the field when

Australia batted first after winning the toss.

Hutton's tactics were to use Trueman in short spells that would not tire him too quickly, thus maintaining his speed as a useful shock tactic against the batsmen. At lunch honours were even with the scoreboard showing Australia at 58 for 2 but during the interval rain fell to put some extra life into the wicket. Both Bedser and Trueman capitalised handsomely on this when play resumed and wickets began to fall regularly. Soon Australia were in a perilous position, having lost seven wickets with just 160 runs on the board.

By dropping catches England allowed the initiative to slip away. Lindwall was the principal benefactor, to the tune of 62 runs and he was the main reason for the last three wickets adding another 115 runs to an otherwise dismal scorecard. Nonetheless, England had still played very well to dismiss Australia for 275 on the first day. In particular, Trueman had much with which to be pleased. His return to Test cricket was more than justified and although his bowling was not outstanding, the form he showed as he polished off the Australian innings was very reassuring. The crowd gave him a warm welcome; he repaid their faith amply with final figures of 24.3–3–86–4 and the wickets he claimed were largely responsible for Australia's first-day dismissal.

While the match was in progress it was widely believed that England's chances hinged on their first innings performance when chasing Australia's modest total. In fact, the reverse applied, but without the benefit of hindsight a full house was packed into the Oval before play began on the second day hoping to see England force home, in convincing style, the advantage already gained. It was a forlorn expectation. The optimistic crowd went home disappointed with England wavering at 235 for 7 and the position was not encouraging. It appeared that whatever superiority England had once held had been thrown away by the batsmen and this was in conditions that were very much against the Australian fielders.

The weather was wretched on the second day. Undeterred, the Australians rose to the occasion splendidly, bowling and fielding in brilliant style. The all-important factor was catching. Whereas England had dropped five chances, Australia grounded only one and the general consensus of opinion was that the Ashes would be returning down under because of this catalogue of errors by the home side.

Surprisingly, before concluding the day in such an apparently poor position, England had begun in fine style. Edrich was dismissed at 37 but then a century partnership ensued between Hutton and May which placed England well to the fore. It was an illusion. Once the breakthrough occurred the state of the game was transformed with Australia assuming full control but much of the blame for this happening lay on England's own doorstep. A negative approach was adopted which produced painfully slow batting and brought England presumably to the brink of doom. Compton spent an hour scraping together 16 while Graveney was almost as long grovelling over a miserable 4 runs. Only Evans and Bailey made any attempt to force the pace and the latter was still at the crease at the close of play, with Lock as his partner. The situation was depressing.

What could have been a match-winning position for England was hanging by the finest of threads. There was very little to separate the two sides but the drama was brought almost to its final act on the third day as England took a stranglehold on the game with some marvellous, and very astute, cricket. In the first instance there was some resolute tail-end batting. Lock was soon dismissed but Trueman, in scoring 10, stayed long enough to help Bailey add 25 for the ninth wicket to take the total to within 13 of the much decreed 275 runs Australia had acquired. Even better things were in store when Bedser joined Bailey for the last wicket. The scoreline progressed by another 44 priceless runs thus giving England an unexpected lead of 31. The indomitable Bailey, principally responsible for the lead, was last out for 60 leaving Bedser undefeated on 22 and it was an extremely purposeful effort for the final two wickets to add 69 invaluable runs with the odds seemingly stacked well against them.

At this stage of the game an important change occurred in the state of the wicket. It was no longer responsive to pace bowling and, consequently, when Australia began batting a second time Bedser and Trueman were allotted just three and two overs respectively. This meant that after only twenty minutes the spin twins Laker and Lock were brought into the attack. In such moments of inspiration are Test Matches, or series, won and lost, for by this brilliant tactical manoeuvre Hutton brought the Ashes back to England. The ploy was masterful. From the moment the slow bowlers began operating the pressure was applied remorselessly and the game belonged to England.

Laker gained instant success, trapping Hassett leg before wicket in his first over. Little more than two hours later the innings was completed. The collapse did not begin immediately for, from 23 for 1, Hole and Morris carefully advanced the score to 59 when disaster struck. The time was 3.15 pm. By 3.29 pm the Australian innings lay in ruins. In those fourteen frantic minutes four wickets fell for the addition of a negligible two runs. Laker and Lock caused the devastation and when the fourth wicket of the ill-fated quartet fell to make the score 61 for 5 Australia's lead amounted to an insignificant 30 runs.

By the tea interval the lead had stretched to 100 runs for the loss of two more wickets. Archer and Davidson decided the time had arrived for more forceful tactics. Defence would pay few dividends with such a slender lead and there were not many alternatives. Laker received some heavy punishment after tea but the policy of the batsmen was always doomed to failure. Hutton counteracted with some swift changes in his field placings and the strategy worked. The last wicket fell with the score standing at 162 after only two-and-a-quarter hours' duration and its speedy conclusion was due entirely to Laker (16.5–2–75–4) and Lock (21–9–45–5) taking full advantage of the turning wicket.

For Trueman, the Australian second innings was his last active participation in the match. He bowled just two overs in the innings but was not totally out of the action, taking two fine catches to add to his four first innings wickets. He had played his part as well as anybody in achieving the victory, which came as certainly as night follows day. The target was 132 runs and in the early afternoon of the fourth day Compton made the winning hit to guide England home to an historic eight wicket win.

The victory was indeed historic. England had regained the Ashes, which Australia had held since 1934, and the victory was the first at home since 1926. Incredibly, the series then had been won by exactly the same margin as in 1953, by one game to nil with four drawn, and the vital victory had been achieved on the very same ground, the Oval. It was almost as long since England had actually won a Test against Australia, let alone a series. At home, the last previous victory had been in 1938 when Hutton made his then world record score of 364 although one victory had been achieved on the 1950–1 tour to Australia after four successive defeats in the same series. The final irony came with the final Test of 1953. Hutton lost the toss then for the fifth time in the series and yet still managed to win the rubber. All in all, it was a remarkable achievement by the England team.

Trueman, still on the threshold of his career, could have experienced few sweeter moments in all his fourteen years in the England side. He had played his part in no small way but, in many ways, it would be as well for him to savour the success while he could. 1953 was the first of only two occasions (from six separate encounters with the Australians) that Trueman would be a member of an Ashes-winning side. The second would be in 1956 when, as in 1953, he did not take part in the whole series, playing only two matches. England retained the trophy when visiting Australia in 1954–5 but Trueman was not even considered for the trip! The Ashes finally went back to Australia after the disastrous tour of 1958–9 and it was not until long after Trueman retired that they were regained.

It all made the Oval 1953 an historic place to be and in some small way would help to compensate Trueman for the bitter disappointments that were to come both in the years ahead and, more importantly, in the not so distant future.

AVERAGES FOR 1953 SERIES *v* AUSTRALIA: Five Tests, Played One

Overs	*Mdns*	*Runs*	*Wkts*	*Ave*
26.3	4	90	4	22.50

Inns	*NO*	*Runs*	*HS*	*Ave*
1	0	10	10	10

Catches=2

Match results=England 1, Australia 0, 4 Matches drawn.

Statistics
1 Total Test wickets=33
2 Total catches=3
3 Total runs=27
4 Total appearances=5

Next on the agenda for England's cricketers was the winter tour to the Caribbean. Although Trueman had not figured prominently in the Ashes series it was obvious he was firmly in the selectors' minds regarding future events. The pointer to this came towards the end of July when MCC announced the names of ten players who would form the nucleus of the party to embark for the West Indies in December 1953. Trueman's name was on the list even though he had yet to play in a Test that summer. The ten chosen were Hutton, Bailey, May, Compton, Graveney, Watson, Evans, Laker, Lock and Trueman. From the composition of this advance party it was plain to see that much store was being placed in Trueman's selection. Bedser had already intimated he would not be making the trip thus limiting further MCC's already small list of suitable candidates for the fast bowling positions.

Of the ten players mentioned only Bailey, in addition to Trueman, was a bowler of any real pace. Offsetting this, was the point that he was going on the tour in the capacity of all-rounder. Under the hot, often oppressive climate of the Caribbean it would be expecting a great deal of the Essex man to both bat and bowl over lengthy periods of time to any marked degree of success. That he would do so on numerous occasions speaks volumes for his cricketing ability and dogged determination.

While the Fifth Test against Australia was in progress the remaining five names necessary to complete the touring party were announced. They were Statham, Moss, Spooner, Wardle and Suttle. This gave the squad a full compliment of four fast bowlers, two left-arm slow bowlers and an off-spinner in Laker placing the emphasis firmly on attack. It was a positive approach to the forthcoming series but a heavy responsibility hung on the shoulders of the five recognised batsmen and much could depend on the efforts of Bailey and Evans if any crises arose. The tour began in December and was Trueman's first trip abroad with MCC. When the time came for the team to return home it was very nearly the last overseas trip he would make and there is little doubt that the tour, plus its aftermath, was to decimate and all but ruin Trueman's Test Match career. First came the Test Matches. They were the primary motive for MCC making the trip and reasons for the sad, sorry affair can come later.

Sabina Park, a tiny picturesque ground with the surprisingly small ground capacity of around 12,000, set the scene for the First Test early in January 1954. MCC had played a number of representative games leading up to the First Test in which Trueman had performed creditably, particularly against Jamaica on the same Sabina Park ground when he had snapped up 5 for 45 in the second innings. From this his selection appeared almost automatic for the Test and the only doubt was whether Moss would gain preference over Laker. This proved to be the case and England went into the game with all four front-line bowlers available: Trueman, Statham, Bailey and Moss.

From a cricketing point of view, everything was working out quite well for Trueman up to this stage of the tour. He had bowled with reasonable consistency but this was to change substantially during the First Test. West Indies batted first and totalled an impressive 417 runs of which Trueman conceded 107. For his efforts he was rewarded with a scant brace of tail-end wickets. A too frequent dispensing of short-pitched deliveries proved to be the root cause of Trueman's downfall and West Indies batsmen took full advantage of them. It was a less than conspicuous baptism into Test cricket in the Caribbean but he showed on the first day's play that he was far from downhearted. On one occasion, when fielding on the boundary, he entertained the crowd delightfully by returning the ball full-pitch to the wicket-keeper with his left hand! On other less serious occasions Trueman has even been known to bowl left-handed with the same apparent ease thus showing the complete all-round cricketing ability he possessed.

In sharp contrast to West Indies, England were in trouble from the start of their first innings. The collapse continued unabated and by the end of the third day the innings was as good as over. The score stood at 168 for 9, a disastrous state of affairs, and the last wicket added only one more run the next day before the innings was summarily closed. Amid great surprise, West Indies did not enforce the follow-on. Instead, an already healthy lead was consolidated and in little more than a day's play the home side added 209 before declaring early on the fifth day. This set England the enormous task of scoring 457 to win.

In reaching 227 for 2 by close of play on the same fifth day, what had once been a highly impossible target began to loom within the bounds of possibility for England. The backbone of this score came from a splendid century by Watson but once May was dismissed for 69 on the last day any hopes of victory disintegrated. From 227 for 2 England plummeted to 316 all out in a woefully inept display of batting but that collapse tells only half of the story. The real collapse began when the score reached 277 and while it staggered up to 285 seven wickets fell. It was only by virtue of a last wicket stand of 31 between Bailey and Moss that 300 was raised but the effort was in vain. West Indies won by 140 runs and if any semblance of success was to be achieved on the rest of the tour a great deal of improvement would be needed in the middle order batting.

As for Trueman, he had effectively bowled himself out of the side. Over-use of the bumper and general lack of direction brought some very disappointing returns. They were 34.4–8–107–2 and 6–0–32–0 for the first and the second innings respectively and it was not to be until the Fourth Test at Port of Spain that he would regain his place in the team.

In the two intervening Tests, played at Bridgetown and Georgetown, England's fortunes fluctuated wildly. The whole tour became shrouded with gloom and despair after a resounding defeat in the Second Test put MCC two down in the series with the uncomfortable yet distinct prospect now facing them of losing the rubber in three straight games. It was not to be. With commendable resilience, England bounced back to win the Third Test at Georgetown in convincing style by nine wickets. The victory put a completely different complexion on the situation and from a once near-hopeless position the future looked decidedly brighter now. The immediate future meant Trinidad, and Port of Spain, for the Fourth Test and the match marked Trueman's return to the side.

The game was played on a wicket covered with jute matting and this, above all else, was responsible for the high-scoring but positively dull draw which ensued. West Indies took first strike and when they batted well into the third day in amassing 681 for 8 declared they gave themselves only one chance of victory. That was to make England follow-on. It would mean bowling England out twice in three days but even if the follow-on could have been enforced it is highly unlikely that, on such a wicket, there would have been sufficient time for this to occur. In the event, the hypothesis was never put to the test but towards the close of England's first innings it was very much touch and go whether or not the follow-on would be saved. When Trueman and Statham came together for the last wicket the score stood at 510 for 9 with the follow-on target still another 22 runs away. To England's delight, they saved the day but it was a close thing. Trueman was last out, lbw to King for 19, with the score at 537 and the follow-on had been averted by just 5 runs. Not for the first, or last, time had Trueman's batting, rather than his bowling, proved invaluable to his side's cause.

Once West Indies had to bat again a draw became inevitable. Their declaration at 212 for 4 was little more than a token gesture and England were not troubled to bat out time, reaching 98 for 3 in the process. A definite result had never looked a real possibility and for Trueman the game had been an inauspicious return to the side. The first innings, he toiled away for 33 overs to claim a solitary wicket for 131 runs and, as in the First Test, he was having to work hard for scant reward. His second innings effort was much better in that his accuracy improved a great deal. Then he bowled 15 overs for 23 runs, again taking one wicket, but the picture forming from these performances was becoming clearer. The every-Test success he

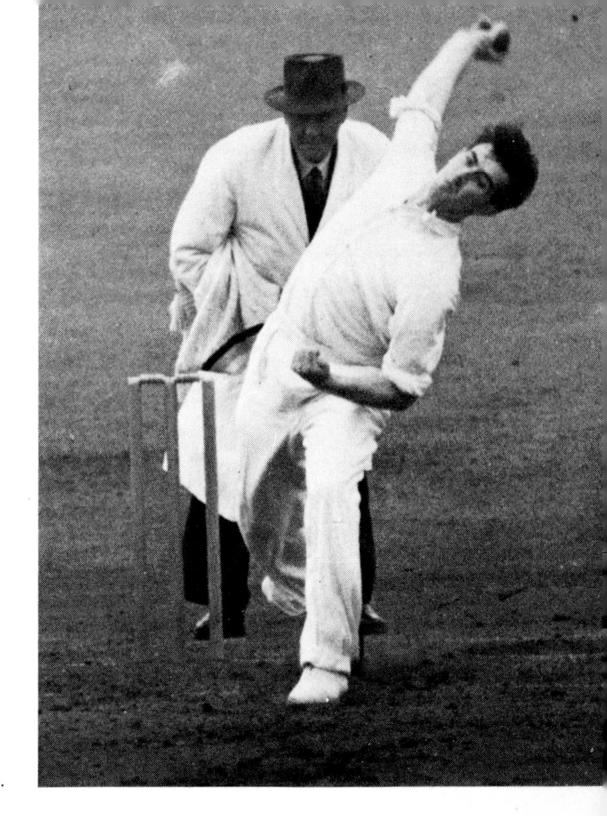

Trueman in action against India at Old Trafford 1952.

G. Langley (Australia) caught by Fred Trueman in the final Test at the Oval, 1953.

The England team that won the ashes, 1953. *Standing left to right*: Bailey, May, Graveney, Laker, Lock, Wardle, Trueman. *Seated left to right*: Bill Edrich, Alec Bedser, Hutton, Compton, Evans.

Pairaudeau (West Indies) is clean bowled by Trueman at Edgbaston in the 1957 series.

had previously enjoyed in his short Test career was eluding him now in the islands of the Caribbean.

From Trinidad it was back to Jamaica, and Sabina Park, for the Fifth Test. If England could somehow manage to win, thereby squaring the series, it would rank as a most praiseworthy achievement after the calamitous start made to the tour. That they did, despite suffering from several handicaps, was made all the more meritorious when considering that the players were now at the end of a long, exacting and often frustrating four-month tour. For the game, the most pressing problem was the absence of Statham through injury. This placed an awesome burden on the shoulders of Bailey who, because of it, was placed in the rare, though not unique, position of being both opening batsman and opening bowler of a Test team. By his very cricketing nature, Bailey was a fighter and a grafter who refused to give in no matter what the odds and the way he rose to the challenge in this particular match must place him high in the all-time list of England's outstanding all-rounders.

In the simplest terms, the match was won and lost on the first day's play. West Indies again won the toss and elected to bat first but incredibly, on a perfectly good batting wicket were dismissed for a meagre 139 runs. In one of his finest-ever bowling performances for his country Bailey wreaked constant, unrelenting havoc among the batsmen and his figures alone tell the story: 16–7–34–7. It was brilliant, deadly bowling of the highest accuracy giving England a stranglehold on the game they never once released. Hutton made sure of that. He scored a magnificent double century in England's first innings total of 414 and from that point onwards the game was safe for England.

West Indies performed infinitely better the second time around but the damage already done was irreparable. A final score of 346 all out was a mere 71 ahead of England and the necessary runs were duly scored with more than a day's play remaining. It was an amazing fightback by England to square the series and the match brought to an end a tour full of rancour, not a little bitterness and a great deal of controversy but the win at Sabina Park did at least give the series an honourable end-result: two victories to each side with one game drawn.

Trueman produced his best bowling of the series in this match, particularly in the second innings when he took 3 for 88 but it was impossible for him to emulate Bailey. He was the real hero. His supreme effort in the West Indies' first innings put England firmly on the road to victory, and at the same time confounded the pundits who had written off England's chances after the two early defeats. Much the same could also be said about Trueman, though to a slightly lesser degree. He made a very disappointing start in the First Test, while his recall coincided with the lifeless jute matting pitch at Port of Spain but the Fifth Test saw him return to something like his true form. His figures for each innings read: 15.4–4–39–2 in the first and 29–7–88–3 in the second innings and they showed a marked improvement on his earlier efforts. Whether or not it had been worthwhile is another matter because that effort was to be his last for England for more than a year.

The tour ended on a victorious note at Sabina Park but it was more than slightly discordant. In one respect, the players could return home with a sense of achievement after their four months in the Caribbean. Very few teams could turn a two-nil deficit into a two-all draw with only three games remaining in a series and the players could feel well pleased at having done so but there the joy ended. The other side of the coin was far less pleasing. Several players would return home feeling quite bitter and resentful at the large amount of bad publicity the tour had attracted. Furthermore, Trueman returned to become a virtual outcast from the England team, and was put on the shelf by the selectors.

The last Test of the West Indies tour had been Trueman's eighth appearance for England. While it was not a great number he had proved in those few games that he had the potential to perform very successfully in Test cricket. Yet, he was not picked again until June 1956 and altogether, in the three seasons following the tour, he gained selection for a paltry three Tests. The obvious question, therefore, is what caused this blatant expulsion from the England team? The answer is neither singular nor straightforward.

In the beginning there was the tour. In retrospect, there can be no shadow of doubt that the 1953–4 MCC tour to West Indies was an ill-tempered and highly contentious affair from start to finish. The reasons for this are numerous and diverse and the full truth will probably never be known. What is certain is that, for Trueman, the tour was nothing short of a personal catastrophe but was the tour, or he himself, so bad that he had to be expelled from the team for nearly four years? In effect, that is what happened because out of the following twenty-six Tests played by England after the tour he was selected only three times and on those occasions it was simply because the selectors had nobody else to whom they could turn. From 1954 until the start of the 1957 season Trueman hardly warranted consideration by the selectors and the whole matter revolves totally around the West Indies tour.

To assess how much blame was directly attributable to Trueman would be impossible but by no stretch of the imagination could he be wholly to blame and certainly not as much as was originally implied. There were several other factors besides Trueman, not least being the organisers, MCC. From the outset they placed members of the party in an invidious position by taking the unusual step of appointing a player-manager to take charge of affairs. This does not reflect on the personal ability or integrity of Mr C. H. Palmer, the man chosen for the post, but the whole charade put him, the players and not least the captain in a most ambiguous set of circumstances. At one time it would mean he was head of affairs dealing with matters or delegating responsibility as he saw fit while the tour progressed. This would cease the moment he stepped on to the field in a match and the balance of power would be reversed. Then it would be his turn to take and obey orders from his captain, Hutton. It was hardly a system guaranteed to sustain perfect harmony over the course of a hard four-month tour.

Moving on to the tour in particular, it became increasingly obvious with the passing of time that a lot of ill-feeling was being generated both on and off the field. Some of this centred around dubious umpiring decisions going against the MCC team in Tests and colony games and several times players were openly seen showing their disapproval of such decisions. Most touring teams, English or otherwise, are apt to make this issue a perennial bone of contention but in West Indies it did appear to bear some justification. Hutton, at one stage, objected to a certain umpire appointed for a match but much could have been done from within the MCC camp to alleviate the problem without the necessity of making it public knowledge. A quiet word, behind the scenes, to some of the more remonstrative players not to allow their emotions to gain the upper hand could possibly have saved some of the incidents occurring which gained so much notoriety.

Perhaps the most infamous of these 'incidents' took place at Port of Spain during the Fourth Test when an umpire alleged he was called a 'black bastard' by an English player. Immediately Trueman was blamed. The umpire did not say it was Trueman but that counted for nothing. To all intents and purposes Trueman was just the right type of man to blame. To be exact, what the umpire did say was that it was one of the Yorkshiremen on the field who made the remark and as there were four at the time it makes a world of difference to the story.

Trueman has always categorically denied that he made any such comment. He had done so consistently and even went so far as to ask Len Hutton, the England captain at the time, about the incident publicly during a television chat show in the late 1960s. Hutton refused point blank to discuss the matter and would neither confirm nor deny that Trueman did not say the ill-fated words. When a person goes to such lengths to prove his innocence, they are not the actions of a guilty man and it is sufficient to say that one ex-England cricketer, whoever it was that did say it, must be devoid of a conscience if the incident has left no mark on him after so many years have passed.

Another direct criticism to be aimed at Trueman was that he behaved in a belligerent manner on the field. Such an idea is sheer hypocrisy. What else is any fast bowler, not just Trueman, but belligerent? When a man runs twenty yards or more building up momentum for the sole purpose of dispatching a five-and-a-half ounce ball with the maximum possible velocity towards a fellow human the act, by simple definition, is belligerent. By way of comparison, when Trueman had been pulverising the helpless Indians into oblivion eighteen months earlier no such accusations were made. And that was at a time when the Indians were reported to be running away from his bowling out of sheer terror.

The critics were not long in sharpening their pencils in readiness to begin the tirade against Trueman. After the tour E. W. Swanton wrote, 'I confess I would not be happy to see his name again in a touring party, irrespective of the number of wickets he may have got, unless I was convinced of a radical change of outlook.'

Trueman may have been a trifle wayward at this stage of his career but he was very young too, at a shade over twenty-three when the tour ended. What a player of that age needs is guidance, not stinging criticism. In its 1955 edition, *Wisden* added its own penetrating comment to the tour stating: 'earlier and firmer handling of the most recalcitrant member, Trueman, might have avoided several situations' and therein lies the crux of the whole matter. Not his captain, Hutton, the MCC, nor even the eminent Mr Swanton, appeared remotely concerned in handing out any such kind of help. And if not guidance, because Trueman was unmanageable on the tour, then MCC had the ultimate weapon at their disposal. They could have sent Trueman home. As this course of action was not taken the obvious inference must be that his behaviour was nowhere near as bad as some people implied at the time. Nevertheless, it made little difference and the best bowling potential seen in England for years would have to make his own way in the game with precious little help from the powers-that-be.

Over the next three years or so that way was to be a lonely one. Only the odd one-off appearances would come Trueman's way as consolation. It would take a long time to regain his place in the England team but he was good enough to do so, solely on merit, and prove his critics even enemies, wrong. However, when the reappearance did finally materialise there is a surprising twist to the tale. England would have a new captain, Peter May. After the Fifth Test at Sabina Park 1954, Trueman would never play for England again under the captaincy of Len Hutton; in the final analysis of Trueman's long sojourn in the wilderness that may well be the most intriguing point of all.

AVERAGES FOR 1953–4 SERIES *v* WEST INDIES: Five Tests, Played Three

Overs	*Mdns*	*Runs*	*Wkts*	*Ave*
133.2	27	420	9	46.66

Inns	*NO*	*Runs*	*HS*	*Ave*
4	1	38	19	12.66

Catches=0

Match results=West Indies 2, England 2, 1 Match drawn.

Statistics
1 Total Test wickets=42
2 Total catches=3
3 Total runs=65
4 Total appearances=8

3 South Africa, at home, 1955 and Australia, at home, 1956

The catalogue of Trueman's omissions from successive England teams over the three years following the Caribbean tour bears a miserable testimony to the attitude of the selectors. Trueman became a Test exile, displaying his talents solely on the county circuit, while England carried out a full programme of Test commitments at home and abroad. It was not until 1957 that Trueman regained his place in the team on a full-time basis (in the home series against the West Indies) and in the interim period England played a total of twenty-six Test Matches. Out of all of these games Trueman played in just three and it constituted the most barren period in his entire career. It was abundantly clear that the selectors did not want to know him at this time but the figures need careful clarification, in relation to appearance and non-appearance, to place the matter in a clear perspective.

The fleeting appearances came with one match against South Africa in 1955 and two matches against Australia one year later. Prior to these series Pakistan had paid their first-ever visit to England for a four-Test rubber in 1954, and England had toured Australia and New Zealand in the winter of 1954–5. As Trueman was completely ignored as a possible candidate for any of these series this immediately took away eleven possible Test appearances he may have been entitled to. Then came a possible breakthrough. Trueman was picked for the Second Test at Lord's against South Africa on their 1955 tour of England (over one year and twelve Tests after his last Test) but it was his only match of the summer. There was no tour taking place from which he could be omitted in the winter of 1955–6, as most certainly would have been the case, and the next visitors due in England were the Australians in 1956. Again, the comeback became a possibility. Trueman gained selection for the Second and Third Tests, a 100 per cent improvement on the previous year, but once more an abrupt halt was called. To finalise the point, any hopes for further honours after the Australian series were positively dismissed when the party chosen to tour South Africa in the winter of 1956–7 was announced. Predictably, Trueman's name was not on the list and this five-Test series brought the total number of Tests played by England up to twenty-six since Trueman's original omission in 1954.

In this period the all-important Ashes series had been won quite convincingly by England which gave the impression that the team was performing well but this was not the case. It was all well and good to be beating Australia but, at the same time, results against lesser countries were not in keeping with this trend. Surprisingly, the babes of Test cricket, Pakistan, had drawn the 1954 series with one victory going to each side. The remaining two series were both against South Africa, at home and abroad, and England's achievements were only moderate. In 1955, in England, the series went to the home side by three games to two while in 1956–7 the series ended all-square at two-all with one game drawn. While all this meant that England had not lost any of the series the fact remains that an alarming number of individual Tests were being lost.

There were some high-spots, notably when Australia were trounced on their territory, three-one, in 1954–5 and both Tests against New Zealand at the end of the same tour were won but the overall picture is not as rosy as it first appears. The full record during Trueman's absence reads P26 W13 L7 D6. The record is fair but no more, and by no stretch of the imagination could it suggest that England were so successful that Trueman was a disposable asset who could be ignored without thought. Yet, that is what happened. Whoever was doing Trueman's job was achieving only a mixed amount of success and the time would come when the selectors would publicly admit this by bringing him back. In the meantime, the general idea was that England had another great fast bowling hope in the shape of Frank Tyson.

Events were to prove this a somewhat forlorn hope but it served as an effective method of keeping Trueman out of the team while Tyson was given his chance. Not that Tyson was not worth a trial—he was, without doubt. Tyson was a very good and genuinely fast bowler who on his day was more than likely faster than Trueman. The manner in which he tore through the Australian batting on the 1954–5 tour gives conclusive evidence of his ability but Tyson lacked one ingredient absolutely vital to all fast bowlers, fitness. Throughout his Test Match career he was plagued by injury and consequently was never on the scene long enough to be considered superior to Trueman. In effect, Tyson burnt himself out and was never able to match Trueman's susteined work-rate and high level of consistency. A perfect example of this comes with Trueman's three appearances during his long spell on the sidelines. On all three occasions Tyson was not fit to play, and in the 1956 series against Australia that was the case until the final Test. By that time the season's work was virtually over.

In terms of making a full-time comeback to the England team it was all a pipe-dream for Trueman. The selectors were toying with him, picking him when there was nobody else available and then casting him aside at the first opportunity. The strategy was doomed to failure for two reasons. First, because Tyson's Test career lasted just four years, 1954–8, and second, because Trueman was simply too good to be overlooked any longer after 1957. The public knew it, the media knew it and the selectors finally had to admit it.

The first reappearance came at Lord's for the Second Test against South Africa in 1955. Possibly, this could have been the springboard to more regular appearances in the future. Several bowlers were injured but it was Trueman's only match of the summer. His selection was nothing more than a stopgap measure and while his performance was hardly outstanding his dismissal after the game was as sudden as his recall. How different to the situation in later years when Trueman's inclusion in the side would be of paramount importance. In 1955 he was used solely because there was nobody else available for one particular match.

On the day Statham was England's hero. Due solely to his efforts in the South Africans' second innings England gained a comfortable 71-run victory. While Trueman toiled away for thirty-five overs in the match to take a meagre two first innings wickets, Statham was turning in his best-ever performance in his Test career. It was a brilliant non-stop piece of fast bowling by Statham and he bowled throughout South Africa's entire second innings which lasted three-and-three-quarter hours. There was a break for bad light on the fourth day and this enabled Statham to return refreshed when play resumed but it detracts nothing from his performance. It was pace bowling of the highest order and his final analysis read 29–12–39–7.

This remarkable effort by Statham highlights a peculiar feature of the long association he and Trueman shared together in the England team. It was always one or the other who took the lion's share of the wickets and it was a very rare occasion when they would demolish the batting side in double harness. Only once, in fact, against West Indies on the 1959–60 tour to the Caribbean. For Trueman, the match was a complete disappointment. His figures in both innings were unimpressive, 16–2–73–2 and 19–2–39–0 respectively, and it was no real surprise when he was omitted for the next Test. That was all for 1955 and the comeback would have to wait another year until once again he would be picked to play at Lord's against Australia.

AVERAGES FOR 1955 SERIES *v* SOUTH AFRICA: Five Tests, Played One

Overs	*Mdns*	*Runs*	*Wkts*	*Ave*
35	4	122	2	61.00

Inns	*NO*	*Runs*	*HS*	*Ave*
2	2	8	6	—

Catches=0

Match results=England 3, South Africa 2.

Statistics
1 Total Test wickets=44
2 Total catches=3
3 Total runs=73
4 Total appearances=9

Accepting that Trueman was not a likely candidate for the rest of the South African series, his next England call-up could have been as early as the First Test against Australia in 1956. Both Tyson and Statham were unfit but the uncompromising attitude towards Trueman persisted and Moss and Bailey were picked as the opening bowlers for the game. When the team for the Second Test was announced the selectors showed that their policy was nothing if not varied. Statham and Trueman came into the side with Bailey retaining his place but not as opening bowler.

The Australians of 1955 vintage were generally acknowledged as one of their weaker sides to visit England but this did not prevent them from gaining an overwhelming victory at Lord's. It was by 185 runs but at the end of the game the Australians had only ten fit men and they had played throughout deprived of the services of their most feared bowler, Ray Lindwall. Nevertheless, it was still enough to see off England's challenge. These points apart, however, Trueman emerged from the game with great credit and in the process reached the first significant milestone in his career, his fiftieth Test wicket.

The game would be three days old before that singular event occurred. In the prior events Australia won the toss and decided to bat first. They reached 180 for 3 on an opening day which was curtailed by bad light but the signs were already apparent that they were assuming command. On the second day, Trueman bowled very fast, much faster than had been seen for some time, but his direction was a little wayward and there was a tendency to bowl too short. In spite of this he gave away fractionally less than two runs an over in the course of the Australian innings. It closed at 285 all out with Trueman showing the respectable analysis of 28–6–54–2. In addition to this, he also took a superb catch at second slip, swooping effortlessly on the ball to enhance his ever-growing reputation as a first class close-in fielder.

In comparison to Australia's batting display, England positively floundered. The total required for the first innings lead was a moderate one by Test standards but England failed to approach within 100 runs of it. The only noteworthy contribution came from skipper Peter May, who made 63 as the rest of the innings fell apart around him to close at 171. The position was far from good but, with the aid of a magnificent spell of bowling by Trueman, England scraped back into the game.

It happened on the third day. Where he had previously been criticised for bowling too short Trueman now kept the ball well up to the bat. In a marvellous piece of very fast, hostile bowling that lasted for fifteen overs he accounted for the wickets of Burke, Harvey, Burge and Miller. Of the four, the dismissals of Harvey and Miller bore a special significance but for two widely-differing reasons. First came Harvey's demise. It was off a genuine, full-blooded leg-glance and Bailey, at leg-slip, flung himself full length to take a stupendous mid-air catch that bordered on the miraculous. Next came Miller, the last of the four victims for the day, and when he was walking back to the pavilion Trueman had reached his half-century of Test wickets.

K. R. Miller c Evans b Trueman

The figure had come up in his tenth Test, no mean achievement, and he finished the Australian second innings with one more wicket on the fourth day for final, splendid analysis of 28–2–90–5.

The total required by England to win was a considerable 372. It was not impossible but when four wickets fell before 100 was reached the game was as good as lost. With the score at 186, Trueman was the unfortunate last man out. This second effort was little better than the first and on the day England had been soundly beaten by the better side but from Trueman's point of view he could glean much satisfaction from his own performance. The comeback was well and truly under way now. After taking seven wickets at Lord's it would be impossible to drop him for the Third Test at Headingley but that was where the trail ended.

England won the game by a massive innings and 45 runs, to draw level in the series at one game all and it was made possible entirely by the spinning prowess of Laker and Lock who reaped a rich harvest of wickets on a turning pitch. Between them they claimed a total of eighteen wickets in the match. This left little room for Trueman to shine (or do anything wrong) and he bowled a mere nineteen overs in the course of both Australian innings. He claimed the wicket of opener McDonald each time at a cost of 40 runs but it was to be his last effort of the summer. For the Fourth Test he was relegated to twelfth man.

In all fairness, there can be no disputing the decision taken for the Fourth Test. The state of the wicket justified it and the simple description 'Laker's Match' sums up events perfectly at Old Trafford. Jim Laker bowled himself into cricketing immortality by taking an incredible nineteen wickets in the match: 9 for 37 in the first innings and 10 for 53 in the second. It was a story-book performance which belies description and one that must surely remain an all-time record. A very unique set of circumstances indeed will be necessary for it ever to be broken.

Once omitted from the team Trueman could not regain his place. Tyson was fit again for the final Test, for the first time that summer, and well though Trueman had bowled at Lord's his place went to the Northamptonshire player. Worse was to follow with his exclusion from the party to tour South Africa in the winter under Peter May. No matter how he performed it was not enough, at this stage at least, to impress the selectors sufficiently to consider him for an overseas trip. This was hardly surprising under the circumstances. It was taking Trueman all his time to get a game at home, let alone abroad, so he would have to bide his time before returning to Test cricket.

AVERAGES FOR 1956 SERIES *v* AUSTRALIA: Five Tests, Played Two

Overs	*Mdns*	*Runs*	*Wkts*	*Ave*
75	13	184	9	20.4

Inns	*NO*	*Runs*	*HS*	*Ave*
3	0	9	7	3.00

Catches=4

Match results=England 2, Australia 1, 2 Matches drawn.

Statistics
1 Total Test wickets=53
2 Total catches=7
3 Total runs=82
4 Total appearances=11

4 West Indies, at home, 1957

1957 had to be the make or break year for Trueman. The balance of his entire Test Match career lay in the merits or otherwise of his performances against West Indies that summer and it would either be relaunched once and for all or finished completely. By way of change, Trueman's destiny was, for once, entirely in his own hands for there was now no question of him gaining just the odd appearance. He would play in all five Tests and that put the onus firmly on Trueman's own shoulders. If he did not meet with success future selection for England would have been no more than a flight of fancy but fortunately, both for Trueman personally and England's future generally, failure was never a possibility. Instead, Trueman could begin in earnest the stern task of proving his critics wrong and 1957 effectively marks the real beginning of his Test Match career.

History portrays the 1957 West Indies team as one of the weaker sides to visit England from those islands but it was far from being a poor one. The captain was John Goddard, a vastly experienced cricketer whose only slight disadvantage was his age. At thirty-eight he was rapidly approaching the veteran stage of his career but in terms of experience this made his presence invaluable. The side was a mixture of youth and more senior players and while the results were not very encouraging, especially in the Test Matches, it was plain to see that a great deal of potential lay in the side. Quite a number of setbacks would have to be endured but this was the basis of a brilliant all-round team that would emerge from the Caribbean in the early 1960s and then West Indies would rightfully be one of the premier teams in world cricket.

Prior to 1957 West Indies had enjoyed a plentiful proportion of success against England and had not lost any of the three previous series. These stretched as far back as 1947–8 when West Indies triumphed by two victories to nil in a four-Test rubber on their own soil. Two years later they enjoyed a similar margin of victory, though by three games to one, when they thrashed England on a highly successful tour. As was described in Chapter Three the situation began marginally to improve for England when they returned to the Caribbean in 1953–4 and earned a two-all draw in the series and now, in 1957, came the opportunity to carry on the good work begun some three years before in the latter stages of the last tour.

Throughout the summer the splendid recovery initiated by England in the Caribbean was carried forward in a most convincing manner. Defeat was not even a remote possibility and only in one fleeting instance during the First Test did West Indies have a semblance of a chance of gaining a victory in any of the five Tests played. Indeed, the tourists were rather fortunate not to lose the series five-nil, had fate been a trifle more benevolent to England, but a three-nil winning margin was more than good enough to compensate for two drawn games. By this resounding win in the rubber England established a masterful superiority over West Indies which was not to be relinquished, at home or abroad, until 1963.

With the series heralding the return of Trueman to the England fold it was ironic that West Indies should provide the opposition. After his repeated omissions in previous seasons, brought about entirely by the furore caused in West Indies on MCC's last tour there, it gives the tale an odd look that they should be Trueman's opponents now that he was making a full-time return to Test cricket. It is a strange paradox but it serves to show that whatever occurred on the 1953–4 tour must have been highly exaggerated.

So much for the past. Official recognition, if not blessing, had returned to Trueman and he did not let the opportunity pass him by in 1957. He was successful but it did not come in the same spectacular form as was seen in his only other full home series five years earlier against India. What was evident now was a marked degree of consistency, giving ample proof of Trueman's growing maturity as a fast bowler. In the intervening years from 1954 he had not only learnt his craft well but was also beginning to master it. His talents were put to a far more judicious use than in previous seasons and only in the final

Test, when the slow bowlers had the stage all to themselves, did Trueman fail to take less than four wickets in a match. Consistency was the keynote and Trueman was an infinitely better bowler for it.

Edgbaston, England's lucky ground, was the setting for the series to begin. An unbeaten record in Tests played at the Warwickshire headquarters stretched back over many decades and the long run was to continue unabated. At one stage the sequence was in grave danger of being terminated but a brilliant recovery by May and Cowdrey averted disaster and saved the game for England. May decided to bat first when he won the toss but his side made a miserable start and were in immediate trouble. It was shades of 1950 all over again as Ramadhin struck fear into the hearts of every batsman. He and Valentine had been the most lethal spin combination in the world on their previous visit and were largely responsible for the West Indies success in 1950. Seven years later at Edgbaston the situation was almost identical. Weaving his intricate spell of magic the mercurial West Indian tore England's first innings apart to claim 7 for 49 out of a meagre total of 186 all out.

Poor as the score was it would have been considerably less had not Trueman and Evans staged a valiant face-saving stand of 55 for the ninth wicket. The score was 130 for 8 when Trueman went to the crease and his unbeaten 29 greatly improved the situation, taking the total nearer to 200 rather than the 150 or less that appeared more likely. Even with this valuable tail-end contribution England were still in serious trouble and West Indies emphasised the point by compiling a comparatively large first innings total of 474 all out.

The highlight in the West Indies effort came from Ollie Smith, a brilliant swashbuckling batsman who hammered 161 off the luckless England bowlers. How sad it was that two years later in 1959 he received fatal injuries in a tragic car accident at the age of twenty-six when his best cricketing years still lay ahead of him. Cricketers of Smith's calibre are seen all too rarely and his untimely death came as a bitter blow to cricket lovers the world over. Smith's innings was the basis of a big West Indian lead which eventually stretched to 288 runs and with the tourists in such free-scoring form there was scant

nith (West Indies) is caught
/ Godfrey Evans off
rueman's bowling, 1957.

Trueman batting at Edgbaston during the '57 series versus the West Indies.

Goddard (South Africa) dismissed for a 'duck' by Trueman in the third Test, 1960.

Trueman swings the bat in England's first innings against the Australians at Edgbaston, 1961.

reward for the bowlers. Trueman worked his way through thirty overs to claim two wickets for 99 runs and the position for England was beginning to assume alarming proportions.

Victory was a virtual impossibility and the only hope was to score enough in the second innings to deny the visitors a chance of forcing a win but when the third wicket fell at 113 all hope seemed lost. Rather than the hoped-for draw an innings defeat became an imminent possibility until, with the loss of the third wicket, a rare piece of Test Match drama began to evolve. It was the one piece of Test Match magic that happens perhaps only once every twenty years or so and by it the game was completely transformed, taking away the only chance West Indies would have of defeating England in the whole five-match series.

The turning point came when Colin Cowdrey walked out to join Peter May at the fall of the third wicket. From that moment onwards England were safe. In a remorseless, run-hungry partnership the two men plundered the bowling unmercifully to the tune of 411 runs. Records fell like ninepins as the stand flourished and when it finally ended only two higher stands had been made in the history of Test cricket. These were of 451 by Bradman and Ponsford (Australia) for the second wicket against England at the Oval in 1934 and 413 for the first wicket by Mankad and Roy (India) against New Zealand at Madras in 1956. The individual scores for May and Cowdrey were 285 not out and 151 and May could quite easily have joined the select band of men to have scored a triple century in Test cricket. Instead, he forsook personal ambition and called a halt to proceedings when the score reached 583 for 6.

Of all the long-suffering West Indian bowlers Ramadhin was the most unfortunate. In the innings he bowled an incredible ninety-eight overs, far more than had ever been bowled before in a Test innings and, sadly, the experience was altogether too much for him. Never again was he a force to be reckoned with on the same scale as he had been previously, and, effectively, May and Cowdrey played Ramadhin out of the Test Match spotlight. He was a very fine exponent of spin bowling but after his soul-destroying spell of ninety-eight overs his powers diminished drastically.

May's declaration veered sensibly towards the side of caution, leaving West Indies to score 296 to win in little more than two sessions' play. With a little more time England would almost certainly have won but no blame can be attached to May for this failing to occur. Nobody in their wildest dreams could have envisaged the startling West Indies collapse which ensued but that is precisely what happened and when stumps were drawn they were tottering at 72 for 7. Trueman was allotted a mere five overs in this second, sufficient for him to claim 2 for 7, before giving way to the slow bowlers and but for a shortage of time England would have clinched a victory. Whether or not the outcome was a formality, it was not to be and West Indies hung on grimly for a draw.

At this time May received an unfair amount of adverse criticism for delaying his declaration too long, and in doing so allowed a possible victory chance to slip away. This was totally unjust and under the circumstances his decision was one which the majority of captains would have taken. When considering the many fluctuations of fortunes during the game England had actually done very well to emerge with a draw at the end of it all, without the critics saying they ought to have won. It was only in the last few hours that West Indian wickets began to tumble with alarming regularity and that was a totally unexpected, unforeseen turn of events. Equally surprising was England's remarkable recovery initiated by May and Cowdrey when an innings defeat appeared more likely. Their monumental partnership saved England from defeat, the prime object of the exercise, and the lion's share had come from the captain himself. The critics would have been better disposed to thank May for his splendid rescue act rather than admonish him for being too careful. Far better the man who is cautious but safe than the gambler who loses all.

In the Second Test at Lord's, there was never any suggestion of a gamble. England gained a comprehensive victory by an innings and 36 runs and their supremacy was unchallenged from the first day's play. West Indies batted first on a very green pitch, admirably suited to pace bowling and throughout the innings only three bowlers were used: Bailey, Trueman and Statham. Their dominance was overpowering, especially Bailey, and the tourists were tumbled out for a paltry 127. On the 1953–4 tour Bailey had routed West Indies in the Fifth Test with a magnificent piece of bowling which earned him 7 for 34 and this action replay varied only in the number of runs scored off his bowling. Bailey's haul was 7 for 44 on this subsequent occasion, a marvellous performance, and the innings was completed with sufficient time left on the first day for England to make 134 for 4 in reply.

The England innings eventually stretched to 424 all out and Trueman once again enjoyed a carefree tail-end fling with the bat to better his First Test effort by scoring 36 not out. While he was not running amok in a wicket-taking sense in the series Trueman was still providing a fine service to his side by scoring some decidedly useful runs. West Indies totalled 261 in their second innings but it was far from sufficient and England were not troubled to bat again to ensure victory. Bailey was again to the fore, taking his match tally to eleven wickets while for Trueman it was less spectacular. Two wickets in each innings plus his sound batting contribution was steady if nothing else but better things were in store for Trueman in the immediate future.

The teams moved on to Trent Bridge for the Third Test where the positions were reversed and England batted first. By the end of the first day a large total was already in prospect with the score standing at 360 for 2. This was nearly doubled before May eventually declared at the mammoth total of 619 for 6 on the second day with Graveney notching the second double century of the series. He scored an immaculate 258 with a constant flow of graceful strokes. On his day Graveney was without doubt one of the most stylish and elegant batsmen in the game. The second day ended with mishap for the tourists and they advanced to 59 without loss in reply to England's huge score.

The third day was equally benign to West Indies. They moved sedately on to 295 for 3, with opener Worrell in complete control on 145 not out and with just two days remaining a draw appeared to be a foregone conclusion. Up to this point Trueman had made little impact with not a solitary wicket to his credit. Then came one of his characteristic bursts which changed the entire complexion of the game on the fourth day.

In a spirited attack on the batsmen Trueman tore at them to such effect that he claimed five wickets for a mere 11 runs as the last seven wickets fell for the addition of 77 runs. Trueman's final analysis was 30–8–63–5, a splendid piece of hostile, shock bowling (rather than a sustained spell) and it was the means by which May was able to enforce the follow-on. The one man Trueman failed to dislodge was Frank Worrell. He carried his bat right through the innings to score a chanceless 191 not out and in doing so became the first man since Hutton, who achieved the same feat at Adelaide in 1951, to bat through a complete Test innings.

When close of play came on the fourth day England were well in control. West Indies, requiring 247 runs to make England bat again, were faltering on 175 for 5 and with a full day's play left defeat was staring them in the face. But that was not how Goddard and Smith viewed the situation. On the last day, they defied the English bowlers for three hours forty minutes in a stand of 154 and when eventually the innings closed at 367 all out England had only an hour left to score 121 for victory. This blend of experience and youth had thwarted England's chances in an outstanding partnership of defensive batting and the target was never a viable proposition for England. With half an hour remaining 80 were still required and the second draw of the series became inevitable.

England paid the penalty in the Third Test for playing only four front-line bowlers. This placed an abnormally heavy burden on the shoulders of Trueman and Statham and between them in the match they were required to send down 135 overs. On the final day May became so desperate he was reduced to asking Graveney and D. V. Smith to bowl and England's strike force was brought down to the level of festival cricket. In fact, the match brought Trueman's best returns of the series, 5 for 63 and 4 for 80, but neither he nor Statham could be expected to perform at maximum efficiency with so much bowling thrust upon them. Trueman was back but he was still going to fight very hard to win any praise while present moods persisted and he could be excused for wondering just what he had to do to become a fully accepted England cricketer again.

The series continued with the Fourth Test at Headingley

towards the end of July and England resumed their winning ways. Similar to the first victory the margin was by an overwhelming innings and from it the true picture of the series was beginning to emerge. Play extended only two-and-a-half hours into the third day during which time West Indies were bowled out twice and England batted once to score sufficient runs to negate the necessity to bat again. West Indies batted first to gain once more the dubious distinction of being dismissed in less than one day's play. They were always struggling but the final collapse was as dramatic as anything seen in a Test Match for a good many years.

The crucial time came when the tourists were wavering at 135 for 5. The new ball was due at this juncture and May wasted no time in availing Trueman with it. Minutes later the innings was over. Trueman began the rapid procession of batsmen by bowling first Pairaudeau, then Smith to claim his two wickets of the innings. He did not have time to take any more wickets because Peter Loader stepped up to bowl the next over and with the first three deliveries finished off the innings. The performance was quite stunning and he was only the second Englishman ever to achieve a Test hat-trick in England. Trueman had a hand in the affair, literally, by catching Ramadhin, the second victim, at square-leg and Loader's magnificent trio read as follows:

J. D. Goddard		b Loader	1
S. Ramadhin	c Trueman	b Loader	0
R. Gilchrist		b Loader	0

It was a spectacular conclusion for Loader (who was destined to play only thirteen times in all for England between 1954–9) and England set about making up the deficit of 142 runs. This was done without much difficulty but a final score of 269 all out presented West Indies a far from substantial total to make in return and ensure England had to bat again. It amounted to some 137 runs, a score which should present few problems to any Test side but it was altogether too much for West Indies. Their second innings closed at 132 all out giving England an impressive victory by an innings and 5 runs. In this second batting debacle lies the clue to the West Indies failure in 1957.

Their batting strength was simply not good enough, a fact graphically illustrated in the final Test.

Again Trueman had a fairly quiet match by his standards. Following his 2 for 33 in the first innings he took 2 for 42 in the second but it highlighted his new-found consistency with great clarity. This was the third time in four Tests he had taken four wickets in a match (and every time in the same manner, two in each innings) and allied to his nine wickets in the Third Test he had a total of twenty-one for the series to date. Also he was proving to be far less expensive than in the past and Trueman was now displaying greater all-round strength in his bowling as he grew in experience and stature.

While the batting standards of West Indies had been poor at Headingley they became absolutely deplorable at the Oval in the Fifth Test. There was nothing to show what was in store as England batted first and with centuries from P. E. Richardson and Graveney 412 runs were calmly collected. Trueman was enjoying his best-ever series with the bat and he too added 22 to his previous scores and, in fact, it was the only occasion out of four innings that he was dismissed in any of the five Tests. West Indies took the crease on the second day; by 2.30 pm on the third the match was over and their totals in both innings were their lowest ever recorded in England.

First they were dismissed for a miserable 89 runs, in itself a record as West Indies lowest score in England but in the second innings it was even less albeit by only three runs. Laker and Lock, the supreme spin kings in the world, at that time, worked their way through the batting order with such rapidity that the situation almost reached farcical proportions. It was bad enough with 89 all out but to follow it with 86 all out was a humiliating experience for the immensely talented Caribbean cricketers but against bowlers in such devastating form, especially Lock, there was nothing the batsmen could do. When the final wicket fell the victory margin was an immense innings and 237 runs and Lock had completed his finest-ever Test analysis. The full figures for both bowlers read as follows:

Laker	1st	23–12–39–3	Lock:	1st	21.4–12–28–5
	2nd	17–4–38–2		2nd	16–7–20–6

There was little work for Trueman to do. Five overs in each innings was negligible and he added just one more wicket to his credit for 28 runs. It gave him twenty-two for the series, easily the highest wicket-taker for either side and on the whole the summer of 1957 had been highly satisfactory for him.

England had played a very successful home campaign against West Indies but the task was made so much easier by the tourists' largely ineffective batting. On six occasions out of ten they failed to reach 200 runs and in that lay the root cause of all their problems. Conversely, for Trueman, his problems seemed to be over. His first full series for five years had shown the vast improvement he had made in the interim period. Greater accuracy, consistency and, above all, control gave the lie to alleged reasons for his successive non-selection in previous Tests. The wait had been a long one before penance was deemed to have been served but Trueman was now an integral part of the England team and he could look forward to happier times in the following seasons. The changes had been frequent in the previous three years in an effort to find a suitable opening attack but nobody had come forward who could match Trueman and MCC had to admit it finally and publicly.

Not only was his bowling a prime pleasure-producing ingredient. Trueman finished the series in third place in the batting averages with the unlikely average of 89! This added an extra dimension to his play, that invaluable attribute to a team of a fast bowler normally batting nine, ten or eleven who could score more than useful numbers of runs. 1957 certainly proved Trueman could do that, in addition to taking his fair share of wickets.

The final irony at the end of the series was that MCC had no official tour planned for the winter of 1957–8. This was exactly the same situation as in 1952 when he made his initial breakthrough into Test cricket. Once more Trueman was robbed by circumstances beyond everybody's control of gaining more valuable experience after regaining his place in the team and his next Test chance would have to wait, until the following English season when New Zealand would be the visitors.

AVERAGES FOR 1957 SERIES *v* WEST INDIES: Five Tests, Played Five

Overs	*Mdns*	*Runs*	*Wkts*	*Ave*
173.3	34	455	22	20.68

Inns	*NO*	*Runs*	*HS*	*Ave*
4	3	89	36*	89.00

Catches=7

Match results=England 3, West Indies 0, 2 Matches drawn.

Statistics
1 Total Test wickets=75
2 Total catches=14
3 Total runs=171
4 Total appearances=16

N.B.
1 Trueman's batting average was the highest of his career in an individual Test series.
2 The number of catches Trueman held was the most he took in an individual Test series.
3 Trueman was the highest wicket-taker in the series for the second time in his career.

5 New Zealand, at home, 1958

The summer of 1958 heralded the arrival of the New Zealanders to England, under the captaincy of John Reid, for their fourth such tour since their inception into international cricket in 1929–30. Reid, one of the few truly world-class players to emerge from New Zealand, had been a member of the previous touring party in 1949 when a series of four three-day Tests had been played. The itinerary on this subsequent tour was far more involved and the New Zealanders faced the rigours of a full five-match series with each Test over five days. It was an infinitely more daunting task and whereas the New Zealanders had succeeded in drawing each of the four Tests in 1949 there was to be no similar success in 1958. England overpowered the visitors, dominating them from start to finish, and it was only inclement weather that prevented the home side from gaining a nap hand for the first time in their Test history.

The New Zealanders returned home with a poor record (one of the worst ever recorded by a touring side in England) and not a little adverse, rather unfair, criticism but there were several mitigating factors to offset their dismal performances. Not least was the English weather. The summer was one of the wettest for years and caused so much inactivity in the New Zealand camp that they never really got into any sort of rhythm. Also, cricket six days a week, weather permitting, was a good deal more than the New Zealanders were normally used to playing at home. In a way, this could have aided their cause because the extra amount of cricket may well have afforded them the match practice needed to help the players gain valuable experience. By courtesy of the weather, the theory was not put to the test and when Bert Sutcliffe suffered a nasty arm injury early in the season their problems were complete. Apart from Reid, he was New Zealand's only other accomplished batsman but he was kept out of the game for a month, missing the First Test, and this placed too much responsibility on inexperienced players who were not yet ready to face such pressures.

In the face of such weak opposition it would be reasonable to assume that Trueman would collect a proverbial bagful of wickets in the series but events did not follow such a pattern. Only in the First Test did he gain any substantial reward though the persistent wet weather was hardly conducive to fast bowling. It afforded far greater opportunities to the slower bowlers and Laker and Lock seized their chances with remorseless ruthlessness. Using the pitches and their own considerable talents to the fullest possible advantage the pair succeeded in capturing more than fifty wickets between them in the five Tests.

Lock came top with 34 wickets, followed by Laker with 17 and Trueman came third in the list of wicket-takers with 15 to his name. Under the prevailing circumstances this was a much better achievement than the bare figures would suggest and when taken in context with the complete averages for the series they show up in a much better light. In the five matches a total of 89 wickets were taken by the bowlers of which 66 are already accounted for by Lock, Laker and Trueman. The remaining 23 were fairly evenly distributed among four other bowlers, namely Bailey 7, Statham 7, Loader 6 and Illingworth 3. When considering the initial number claimed by Lock and Laker, Trueman's 15 immediately look far better on two counts. First, it was no mean performance to finish so close to Laker's final tally and, second, he took more than double the number of his nearest colleague.

It would be fair to note that Trueman did play in all five Tests, as against Bailey's four and Statham's two, but he, like the slow bowlers, had to take his chances whenever they arose and as they were few and far between in 1958 his fifteen wickets were not a bad return at all. Trueman did have a little more scope to express himself but he did so nonetheless and that, and the end result, is what matters most.

Following the recently-introduced scheme Edgbaston was the customary venue for the First Test. England were eventual winners by 205 runs, with more than a day to spare, but at first sight this somewhat expected result was far from being a formality. May won the toss and decided to bat but within an hour of the start England were struggling. With only 29 on the scoreboard three batsmen were already back in the pavilion giving New Zealand a splendid start to the series. Then May and Cowdrey joined forces again exactly as they had done so a year previously against West Indies. On that occasion they had shared a record stand of 411 and while the second partnership against New Zealand added considerably less, 121, it was just as necessary to England's cause. Without it, the final total of 221 would have been a forlorn hope but even that, on a good batting wicket, had to be regarded as disappointing.

Where the batsmen had failed, with the exception of May and Cowdrey, Trueman did not. With two hours' play remaining on the first day when they began batting New Zealand were soon reeling. Trueman dismissed opening bat Miller for 7 and by close the score crept at snail's pace up to 41 for 3. Yet, on the whole, this was an excellent first-day performance by the tourists. They were only 180 behind with seven wickets still intact but any hopes of further success were dashed by Trueman on the second morning. The New Zealanders faced him at his very best, not relying solely on speed but bowling with perfect precision and method.

Trueman employed the seam to its maximum effect, swinging the ball considerably both through the air and off the pitch and his fastest deliveries were utilised sparingly. They were more of a shock tactic, a very successful one too, and the ploy worked admirably. In the two-hour morning session England captured six wickets for the addition of a meagre 32 runs and Trueman's share of the spoils was a brilliant 4 for 7. Added to his solitary wicket the previous evening the four gave him a final analysis of 21–8–31–5, easily his best return of the series.

In totalling 94 in their first innings New Zealand narrowly avoided the follow-on. England had to bat a second time and scored 215 for 6 before May declared, setting the New Zealanders the task of scoring 343 to win in two-and-a-half days. Against more formidable opposition this would have been unthinkable but May knew exactly what he was doing. The New Zealanders never looked capable of approaching anywhere near the required total and were bowled out by mid-afternoon on the fourth day. Trueman added just one more wicket to his name in the second innings, at a cost of 33 runs, but his was a sound, satisfactory performance overall. It had been a game of several early fluctuations until Trueman's magnificent spell in the first innings had put paid to any New Zealand hopes of victory and by it the course was set for the rest of the game. Indeed, it was set for the rest of the series and the possibility that the tourists would alter the pattern in any of the remaining Tests was never feasible.

New Zealand's fortunes failed to improve in the Second Test at Lord's and England turned the screw even more in this match, having proceedings speedily finalised with two days to spare despite losing several hours' play because of wet weather on the second day. In fact, it was the weather that was the main instigator of New Zealand's downfall. As at Edgbaston, England batted first but had Reid won the toss events may well have turned out in a completely different fashion. However, Fate did not work its hand in such a fashion and England's first innings score amounted to a reasonable 269 all out.

The weather began to take a hand in the affair before the England innings was concluded. After close of play on the first day it rained so heavily overnight that play on the second day could not start until 3.20 pm, a loss of over three hours. Then, on the resumption, wickets fell with such alacrity that no fewer than thirteen went down in under three-and-a-half hours. First priority for New Zealand was the conclusion of England's innings and this was accomplished with a succinctness not normally seen in their play but few people watching could have envisaged the New Zealanders beginning their second innings before close of play, especially in the short time left before stumps were drawn. Incredibly, this is precisely what happened as New Zealand were shot out for just 47 runs. This was the lowest total ever recorded in a Test Match at Lord's and the fourth lowest in England, only South Africa (30 all out in 1924) and Australia, twice, (36 all out in 1902 and 44 all out in 1896) having previously succumbed for lower scores.

Trueman began the rapid procession of batsmen in and out of the pavilion in his first over by trapping Miller lbw. It was his solitary success of the innings as Laker and Lock took matters in hand. They were practically unplayable, Lock claiming 5 for

17 and Laker 4 for 13, and when New Zealand followed on Lock was equally impressive again. The tourists fared only slightly better at the second attempt, scraping together 74 runs and the margin of defeat was an overwhelming innings and 148 runs. There was hardly any scope for Trueman, though he did pick up 2 for 24 in the second innings but a more interesting point is his hand in dismissing both opening batsmen in both innings. 'A hand' is a quite literal interpretation as the following scorebook entries adequately illustrate.

NEW ZEALAND

	1ST INNINGS			2ND INNINGS		
L. S. Miller	lbw	b Trueman	4	c Trueman	b Loader	0
J. W. D'Arcy	c Trueman	b Laker	14	c Bailey	b Trueman	33

It was a novel, though not unique, way to dismiss two opening batsmen in both innings and made for four variations on the same theme yet Trueman could claim only two of the wickets as his own. Wretched weather again had a devastating effect on the outcome of the Third Test, at Headingley. Constant heavy rain delayed the start until 2.00 pm on the third day but with only a fraction more than half the allotted time play available England were still able to register an innings victory. For the first time in the series Reid won the toss. On doing so the temptation to ask England to bat must have been very great for the pitch was extremely soft and if the weather held firm over the weekend the wicket, by Monday morning, would probably have lost its sting. Theoretically, New Zealand could have held the whip hand by then.

Tempted or not, Reid decided to bat and in three-and-a-half hours saw his side crumble before Laker and Lock for the third successive time in two Tests. Their total of 67 was also the third successive occasion New Zealand had failed to reach three figures in a Test innings and how Reid will have regretted his decision to bat first. There was a two-fold reason for this. One was purely negative in that allowing for the tactic to fail and

England managing to accumulate a large, or reasonably large, score it would have been no bad thing for it would probably have used up much of the little time available. This would have left New Zealand with the relatively simple task of batting out for a draw. Conversely, when noting that Laker and Lock claimed nineteen wickets between them in the match, even with inexperienced slow bowlers in the side New Zealand would surely have reaped some benefit from fielding first. In the event, when England replied to the tourists' first sad effort they rattled up 267 for 2 and May allowed his bowlers seven hours in which to bowl out New Zealand for a second time when he declared.

In the eighty-five minutes remaining for play on the fourth day England snapped up three wickets. Off the second ball of the second day Sutcliffe fell to Lock and the game appeared cut and dried for England. To the surprise of all and sundry the New Zealanders hung on grimly for the better part of another four-and-a-half hours. Spearheading this dour, defensive struggle were two largely unknown batsmen, Playle and Sparling. Playle gave a particularly resolute display in resisting the attack for three-and-three quarter hours in mustering 18 while Sparling occupied the crease for an hour and fifty minutes in making a similar score. He was last man out, but, pluckily though they played, time was always against the New Zealanders.

The conditions were ideal for Laker and Lock, notably on the last day when the pitch had dried out considerably and was, therefore, much more responsive to spin. To their credit, New Zealand did extremely well to last so long in the second innings and it showed, if nothing else, that they certainly did not lack heart. As far as Trueman was concerned, this was another match where he was largely inactive. Similar to Lord's he bowled very little, only twenty-five overs in both innings, and the solitary wicket left by the spinners was his sparse reward.

Nothing had gone right for New Zealand throughout the season and their misfortunes continued in the Fourth Test, at Old Trafford, without a blessing of any kind in sight. In winning by an innings and 13 runs, England became the first team to win the first four Tests of a series in England. In the

1950s circumstances beyond the control of any captain had robbed England twice of gaining this distinction (against India in 1952 and West Indies in 1957) and now the scene was set for the previously unrivalled feat of a nap hand in all five Tests.

The single factor to benefit New Zealand in the Fourth Test was the presence of the sun. It shone on them as they batted first and was more than likely their main asset in aiding the batsmen compile their highest total of the series. But the weather was in an unmerciful, unrelenting mood. The sunshine was only a brief respite from the more usual rain and after two fine days there was a mere forty minutes' play on the third day while on the fourth play did not resume until 3.00 pm. Despite so many hours being lost to the elements England still had the match safely completed by 2.20 pm on the last day and, as so often in the series, Lock was the tormentor-in-chief.

In the New Zealanders' first innings Trueman did reasonably well, as also did Statham. It was one of the few occasions when they both had a reasonable share of the wickets in the same innings of a Test. New Zealand totalled 267 all out with the pair claiming seven wickets between them and Statham just had the edge over his colleague taking 4 for 71 against Trueman's 3 for 67. England batted soundly to secure a lead of 98 but it was a deficit which ought not to have presented any problems to a Test side, not even New Zealand and when, at close of play on the fourth day, their score stood at 30 for 0 they appeared to be quite handily placed.

The morning session on the last day soon put paid to that notion. By lunch the batting had been torn to shreds and the scoreboard showed New Zealand tottering at 76 for 7. Three overs after the interval the rout was complete. Lock, who bowled from the start of play on the fifth day until the match was finished, was virtually unplayable (he had been for most of the summer) and with Statham as his partner they both had the ball shooting through alarmingly at varying pace and height. Lock's final analysis was 7 for 35 off twenty-four overs, with the New Zealand total once more failing to reach the three-figure mark as the final wicket fell at 85. For Trueman's part, it was a largely uneventful match apart from his three first innings wickets and a catch he held to dismiss New Zealand skipper

Reid. In the second innings he bowled a meaningless two overs and altogether it was a back seat arrangement for Trueman at the present time but he could not begrudge Lock his well-deserved glory.

Being four up in the series gave the Fifth Test no more than an academic interest apart from providing England with the unique opportunity of becoming the first team to make a clean sweep of all five Tests of a series in England. Australia had twice accomplished this feat, on their own soil, in 1920–1 against England and in 1931–2 against South Africa, but the weather, so often England's ally in 1958, prevented any possibility of them emulating their old rivals. Less than twelve hours' play were possible in the entire match, depriving either side of a chance of victory from the outset.

Trueman managed to add two more victims to his total when New Zealand batted first but his best moments came in the English innings. He hit a sparkling 39 not out to record his joint-highest score in Test cricket and but for the declaration by May may well have recorded the elusive maiden Test half-century. Unfortunately, as with the highly prized hat-trick, it was never destined to materialise. Leg-spinner Moir received the worst punishment in this innings, a towering six coming from each of his last three overs. Batting apart, Trueman fell from grace slightly when the tourists batted a second time. He dropped D'Arcy twice, once each off Laker and Lock, when England had a slight chance of winning but it was doubtful if the rare lapses made a vast difference to the result. When declaring with a lead of 58, May left his bowlers only two-and-three-quarter hours in which to force home a victory and even with their palpably weak batting it was highly unlikely that New Zealand would have failed to save the match whether or not either chance, or both, had gone to hand.

Thus ended a most successful yet, in many ways, disappointing series for England. A four-nil victory margin was good by any standards but the miserable weather had marred many games and the New Zealanders were well below England's class, a fact plain for all to see. Had the elements been kinder the New Zealanders might have blossomed more promisingly but it is a question devoid of an answer. In Trueman's case, this was one of his quieter, more subdued periods. After playing in ten consecutive Tests he had reasserted himself as England's leading bowler and a tantalising prospect lay in store in the shape of an Australian tour in the winter of 1958–9 following straight on from the New Zealand series.

Over the two seasons 1957 and 1958 Trueman had become an almost automatic choice for England. However, selectors being what they are, this was by no means guaranteed and the Australasian enterprise would prove to be a stern test for Trueman. The trip would be his first overseas trip with MCC since the ill-fated expedition to the Caribbean some five years earlier and much attention would be focused upon him. The Ashes series would be the opportunity to prove his worth once and for all (at home he was obviously back in favour, and the only question remaining was a trip abroad) and there was an added incentive to act as a spur to him as well.

At the end of the 1958 series against New Zealand Trueman's personal total of Test wickets had risen to ninety. With five Tests to be played against Australia, followed by two more against New Zealand, during the winter surely he could return home with the first prestigious century safely tucked under his belt. He did, but it was a touch and go struggle whether or not he clinched it!

AVERAGES FOR 1958 SERIES *v* NEW ZEALAND: Five Tests, Played Five

Overs	*Mdns*	*Runs*	*Wkts*	*Ave*
131.5	44	256	15	17.06

Inns	*NO*	*Runs*	*HS*	*Ave*
4	1	52	39*	17.33

Catches=6

Match results=England 4, New Zealand 0, 1 Match drawn.

Statistics
1 Total Test wickets=90
2 Total catches=20
3 Total runs=223
4 Total appearances=21

6 Australia and New Zealand, on tour, 1958/9

Prior to embarking on the long sea journey to Australia in the winter of 1958, England had been the holders of the Ashes since 1952 and this, following the barren years of the Bradman era was an uncommonly long time. In all, the period covered three separate series, two in England, 1953 and 1956, and one in Australia during the winter of 1954–5. Trueman had played an important role in the decisive game of the 1953 rubber but his claims for a place on the subsequent 1954–5 tour were completely ignored when the Ashes were retained by a margin of three victories to one. To complete the winning trio in 1956 Trueman again did not figure prominently in the series, playing in only the Second and Third Tests, and perhaps the 1958–9 tour would be his chance finally to have a full tilt at the Australians.

After ten successive home Test appearances, against West Indies and New Zealand, there was no doubting that Trueman was back in the groove. All that remained was his active participation on an overseas trip with MCC and the finishing touch to the intricate mosaic that constituted Trueman's permanent recall to the side would be in place. This was duly accomplished when the party bound for Australia was announced. His name figured prominently on the list and his second tour with MCC became a reality, some five years after his first overseas expedition to the Caribbean and it was only a matter of time before Trueman made his first Test appearance on Australian soil.

The strange aspect of the tour for Trueman was the gruelling amount of work he was expected to do. He missed very few games on the Australian part and none at all when the party moved on to New Zealand yet it was not until the Third Test, at Sydney, that the selectors picked him for a Test.

It was mooted at the time that Trueman was suffering from lumbago. According to not very reasoned opinion this rendered him unfit for the First Test and he was still not quite back to full fitness when the Second Test came along but this will be seen as a ludicrously lame excuse rather than a valid reason. Trueman had taken part in far too many prior games for him not to be, at least, near to peak physical condition. Leading up to the First Test, he played in five out of seven representative matches and was then omitted for the Brisbane game. It was at this stage of the tour that Trueman was struck by a mystery back ailment, diagnosed as lumbago, but it disappeared as mysteriously as it had arrived. Then, following the First Test, Trueman took part in all three representative matches prior to the Second Test only to be dispatched to some quiet corner while the actual Test was played. An amount of match play such as this simply does not lend credence to the opinion that he was not fit. However, the selectors thought otherwise and it was Sydney, venue for the Third Test, that saw Trueman make his Test debut in Australia.

Whether or not Trueman would have made any material difference to the results of either of the first two Tests (both were lost by eight wickets) is a matter of pointless conjecture but the fact remains that by the time he was brought into the side the position of May's men was almost hopeless. The series could well be lost in three straight games and unless something approaching a miracle occurred the Ashes were almost certainly lost. England desperately needed to regain some ground and with Australia going all out for a win as well, the match had all the ingredients necessary for an exciting, tense struggle.

After waiting so long for the opportunity to state his case the match was a frustrating experience for Trueman. He was given very little bowling over the course of the six days with the attack left mainly in the hands of Laker and Lock. May began well enough by winning the toss and immediately decided to bat but the advantage was soon returned to the opposition. Both openers fell with little more than 20 on the board, an event that was occurring with alarming regularity in every Test, and it was left to May and Graveney to set about retrieving the situation. They did so quite well with a minor partnership until disaster struck again. In the space of three overs both fell, in addition to Dexter, and only Cowdrey of the recognised batsmen remained with the scoreboard reading 98 for 5. It was a precarious position but the score at close of play, 190 for 6, gave rise for some hopes of a fight back. It was a very good performance to lose only Cowdrey after the terrible start and he and Swetman added 57 valuable runs for the sixth wicket. With Lock as a partner Swetman remained at the crease to add another 34 runs making the possibility of a reasonable score a far more feasible proposition than had once been likely.

On the second day, rain badly interfered with play, making a start impossible before 4.15 pm. Fifty minutes later the tenth English wicket fell at 219 but not before Trueman made some spirited hitting. He went to the crease when Lock was lbw at 194, lost Swetman at 200 and Laker 2 runs later. That made it 202 for 9 and it signalled the time for Trueman to cut loose. Eleven came off one over from Mackay followed by a prodigious long 6 off Benaud and there the innings ended at 219, with Trueman's share being 18.

Australia had gained a slight advantage for the score was not unduly large but England carried on their fighting performances in the early stages of Australia's first innings.

At one stage three wickets were down for 87. One more then would have made a great deal of difference to the game but O'Neill and Favell began a long stand on the third day which re-established the home side's supremacy for the remainder of the match. During this time the bowling came almost exclusively from Laker and Lock. Out of a total of sixty-eight overs sent down in the day they accounted for fifty-four. Their share was equally divided and Trueman bowled just seven overs all day: four at the start of play, one after tea to allow the spinners to change ends and two near the end. The wicket may have been more responsive to spin but this gave neither him nor Statham any chance to express themselves in a reasonable fashion.

Much the same pattern followed on the fourth day. England gained some limited success in the opening stages, giving rise to unfounded optimism, but another stubborn partnership, in the form of Mackay and Davidson, blighted any hopes of a complete breakthrough. Trueman ended the defiant seventh wicket stand, which realised 115 runs, by bowling Mackay and it made for his only wicket in the match but that apart he was given very little else to do. Australia were eventually all out for 357, a lead of 138, and with exactly two days remaining the best England could now hope for was a draw.

Predictably the openers failed again when play resumed on the fifth day. A failure it was without question but to show just how poorly England was being served in this department the 30 runs put together was the best start to date in the series for the visitors. It was a lamentable state of affairs. Once more it was May to the rescue, this time with Cowdrey, with whom he had achieved so much for England when faced with this recurring type of problem. Their answer on this occasion was 182 runs, for the fourth wicket, and May narrowly missed a century, being bowled by Burke for 92. Cowdrey did achieve the landmark, after spending more than an hour in the nineties on the last day and once it was achieved May immediately declared.

The target set was 150 in 110 minutes, one which Australia made no attempt at reaching. They had little difficulty in batting out time to reach 54 for 2 and the series, if not yet the Ashes, was safe for the home side. As before, Laker and Lock spearheaded the bowling and this summed up the match for the fast bowlers; they were nonentities when it came to practising their art. Compared with the fifty-four overs each bowled by the two spinners, Trueman and Statham had just twenty-two and eighteen respectively over the course of the entire game. When considering the amount of time spent at the crease by the Australian batsmen they never had a chance to get at them. The pitch cannot have been over-helpful to spin, as was thought, or Laker and Lock would have realised their successes at the far cheaper rate of 5 for 107 and 4 for 130 respectively. Variation of attack had to be a vital necessity when the two long, century partnerships were in progress but May showed none at all.

The question of the fate of the Ashes was convincingly resolved at Adelaide, in the Fourth Test, as England crashed to a humiliating ten-wicket defeat. On the morning of the first day Laker tested his spinning finger in the nets and decided it was not fit enough to withstand further gruelling punishment at

Test level. This left England with an awkward formation of attack consisting of four fast bowlers and only one recognised spinner, Lock. This may have had some bearing on the final outcome of the match but, without question, the most significant single factor affecting the result was May's decision to put Australia in to bat after winning the toss. It was a most unusual step to take and, in the event, gave Australia the upper hand right from the start. In all fairness to May, it was one of the very few tactical errors he made throughout his career but it was one which cost England dearly.

The first Australian wicket put on 171 runs, with McDonald going on to score nearly as many himself, 170. At the end of the first day the score stood at 200 for 1, putting Australia in an unassailable position and on the second day, as temperatures soared towards 100°F, England's plight worsened. Apart from the batsmen being in such free-scoring form, England were further hampered when Graveney had to replace Evans behind the stumps who again hurt his already damaged fingers. It was impossible for him to continue but Australia, oblivious to the distraction, moved on serenely to 403 for 6 by the close. The innings finally ended at 476, well into the third day, with Trueman finishing the marathon by bowling Lindwall. Of all the bowlers he emerged with the best figures, his 4 for 90 coming off 30.1 overs. It was a fine, sustained performance (as also was Statham's with 3 for 83) and in the latter stages of the innings Trueman had a magnificent spell of 3 for 22, a marvellous feat of endurance in such hot, oppressive conditions towards the end of a very long, tiring stint in the field.

One of the victims was century-maker McDonald and it came after one of the most notorious incidents of the match. One of the umpires for the match, McInnes, had already been involved in several controversial decisions throughout the series but this one caused by far the most uproar. It occurred because McDonald required the assistance of a runner. Burke was the man chosen for the post and in the course of proceedings decided to position himself at point when McDonald was taking strike, rather than the more usual square-leg position. McDonald pushed a ball from Tyson towards Statham at extra-cover and Burke went for the run. Unfortunately,

McInnes moved to the off-side in anticipation of Statham's return to the bowler's end and when the wicket was broken with no runner in sight the umpire immediately said 'Out'. What, in fact, happened was that Burke arrived in line with the crease behind the umpire; therefore McInnes was not in a position to give any decision. There was a very confused, agitated scene on the pitch which resulted, to England's chagrin, in McInnes reversing his original decision and giving McDonald not out. McDonald himself resolved the situation by more or less throwing his wicket away, lashing out wildly and missing a ball from Trueman but it did little to stem the flow of criticism about the umpires.

By way of contrast to Australia's effort, England's innings was one long tale of disaster. In keeping with tradition the openers failed yet again. Only Cowdrey and Graveney showed any willingness to resist with a stand of 96 and this was followed by a total collapse until Watson and Statham showed what could be achieved with a last-wicket stand of 52. This made the score respectable, 240 all out, but England still had to follow on 230 behind and when the second innings started the openers, for once, did not fail. The law of averages had to mean that a good start would come at sometime or other and the 89 realised by Richardson and Watson was the best of the series for England.

May carried on the good work with a well-made innings of 59 but his side was always fighting an uphill battle and wickets fell too regularly for England to deliver an effective challenge. At the start of the last day, 38 runs were still required to make Australia bat again. It was not many runs but with half the side already out and England possessing a more than usual proportion of tail-end batsmen the prospects were bleak. The one spark of a recovery came from Graveney and Tyson, who added 46 for the eighth wicket, but it was all to no avail. The innings closed at 270, setting Australia the facile task of scoring 35 to win in two hours which they duly accomplished without losing a wicket.

A personal failure on the part of Trueman came in this Fourth Test with the registering of his first pair in Test cricket. Happily, it was to be the only pair in his Test career but as he had previously made nought in the second innings of the Third Test, Trueman had the dubious distinction of achieving three successive noughts in consecutive Tests and that was one kind of hat-trick he did not want!

A lead of three games to nil was an impressive scoreline for Australia to take to Melbourne for the final Test. In 1950–1 the position had been slightly worse when the first four Tests were all lost but England managed a victory in the Fifth Test to regain some lost pride. The position in 1958–9 meant nothing short of a victory could save England from their heaviest defeat since 1920–1 when all five Tests had been lost. There was to be no repetition of events nine years earlier and with a defeat by the margin of nine wickets England's comprehensive four-nil hammering was complete.

The side England selected for the Test could have named itself, so acute had the injury problem become. To add to the tale of woe, Statham and Loader were added to an already depressing injury list following a car accident prior to the Test. Fortunately, they were not too seriously injured, but sufficiently so to incapacitate them for some time and necessitate their return to England. This also meant the pair would miss the last part of the tour in New Zealand.

The main front-line bowling was now solely in the hands of Trueman and Tyson, placing an onerous responsibility on their shoulders. Much could depend on their reaction to the situation but their assault on the Australian batsmen was delayed somewhat because, although Benaud won the toss, he decided to follow May's previous example and ask the opposition to bat. The vital difference came in the result. Whereas May's ploy was an abject failure, Benaud's gamble paid handsome dividends. England's first wicket fell without a run on the board, the second at 13 and from that point a recovery was always a hope rather than an actual event. The nearest approach to this was a resourceful eighth wicket stand which yielded 63 runs from Trueman, 21, and Mortimore, 44. It hoisted the score towards some semblance of respectability and as the pair were still together at the end of the first day, on 191 for 7, there was room for a little overnight optimism. Off the second ball of the second morning it faded abruptly with Treman's dismissal. Soon the innings was complete with England's total a moderate 205 all out.

When the Australian innings began, both Trueman and Tyson tested the openers in a lively burst of bowling without being able to gain a wicket. One may well have been forthcoming when McDonald reached 12. In very unusual circumstances, the leg-bail was seen to be on the ground after McDonald glanced Trueman very finely down the leg-side. Swetman, who was standing well back, appealed immediately he noticed the anomaly. The umpire at Trueman's end was not prepared to commit himself, and referred the matter to his colleague at square-leg. Once again controversy reared its head and the conclusion was a not out verdict.

The first wicket was not far away, notwithstanding these strange events. Burke jabbed defensively once too often at a rising ball from Tyson and Trueman gratefully snapped up the chance at short-leg. In spite of this setback Australia began to coast along until they reached 83 for 1, at which point Trueman stepped in to produce one of the electrifying, explosive bursts that was feared by so many batsmen. Harvey was the first to suffer, misjudging a ball that rose more than expected and he was well taken behind the wicket by Swetman. This brought O'Neill to the wicket and off the very next ball Trueman had done it again. The ball pitched about the middle stump, moved away slightly to the off and went like a rocket off the edge into the safe hands of Cowdrey in the gully. Suddenly, the picture had changed very dramatically.

Up until the tea interval Australia were struggling, only to be let off the hook by an inexplicable decision by May. Instead of maintaining the pressure with Trueman and Tyson when play resumed, May opened out with Laker and Bailey. It was a strange mode of attack and Trueman was not recalled until twenty minutes from the close. By that time the danger had passed for the fourth wicket pair. They had been allowed ample time to settle in again and gamely though Trueman tried he was unable to make any further impression. When he came up to bowl the final over of the day McDonald was on 96. Trueman's first response was a bouncer. McDonald retaliated by taking two off the fourth ball but any hopes of reaching his century faded instantly. Four successive bouncers flew from Trueman's hand, bringing forth howls of protest from the crowd but it mattered little. McDonald would still get his century on the third day and Trueman had shown he still retained his spirit at the end of a hard day in the field.

The innings drew to a close on the third day with Australia reaching 351, a lead of 146. Trueman's bowling had been fast and hostile throughout and he finished with figures of 25–0–92–4. In addition to his bowling Trueman also held three catches to round off a fine all-round display in the field and it continued when England batted for a second time. The amount of runs required to make Australia bat again was neither large nor small by Test standards but so weak-willed was England's batting that Australia were always master of the situation and never in danger of losing the match. Only Graveney, 54, Cowdrey, 46 and Trueman with 36 showed any resourcefulness and when the sixth wicket fell at 142 the game was as good as finished. The score slowly crept ahead of Australia while wickets fell regularly until 182 for 9 was reached. At this Trueman decided to take the law into his own hands. He launched into a blistering one-man counter-attack and really opened his shoulders with some astonishing hitting. In the onslaught which followed Davidson was hammered for 14 in one over with some mighty blows that would easily have been sixes on smaller Test grounds. Not content with three boundaries off Davidson, he took one each off Benaud and Rorke before the latter brought matters to a halt by bowling him and completing the innings at 214 all out. The 36 runs he scored was a last despairing, defiant gesture and was the highest score he made to date in his appearances against Australia.

Australia needed a mere 69 runs to win. Early on the fifth day, for the loss of Burke, McDonald scored the winning run and the series was over to give Australia their biggest winning margin, four-nil, since 1920–1. The tour had been a tale of chapter upon chapter of disaster for England. Injuries, poor form and varying standards of umpires all played a part in the defeat but there could be no complaints. They had been well and truly beaten on the day. It was too late to look back, the future was more important and that meant New Zealand.

The one consolation for Trueman at the end of a tour, which brought him more hard work than anything else, was that now he was back in the side he was embarking on the most consistent part of his career in terms of selection. Although he did not realise it, the Third Test at Sydney marked the beginning of a run of twenty-four consecutive appearances for England that would continue until August 1961. There was the proof at last that he had laid the bogey of the selectors. Furthermore he fully justified this long list of appearances by taking over 100 Test wickets in those twenty-four matches.

AVERAGES FOR 1958–9 SERIES *v* AUSTRALIA: Five Tests, Played Three

Overs	*Mdns*	*Runs*	*Wkts*	*Ave*
87	11	277	9	30.77

Inns	*NO*	*Runs*	*HS*	*Ave*
6	0	75	36	12.50

Catches=3

Match results=Australia 4, England 0, 1 Match drawn.

Statistics
1 Total Test wickets=99
2 Total catches=23
3 Total runs=298
4 Total appearances=24

There was a short, five-match itinerary arranged for the New Zealand part of the trip, including two Test Matches. Trueman's first priority was a solitary wicket in either of the Tests. Such singular success would then raise his total of Test wickets into three figures and the first major milestone would have been reached. On the face of it, it appeared to be an odds-on certainty but events ran a more difficult course than that would suggest. In the game immediately prior to the First Test Trueman ran riot through the bewildered Otago batsmen to record one of the best first-class analyses of his career and so suggest there would be easy pickings for him in the Test. The match was played at Dunedin and he collected an amazing thirteen wickets for 79 runs in the two innings. A return of 10–2–34–5 was a good enough effort in the first innings but it was made to look insignificant when compared with figures of 18.3–5–45–8 in the second innings. Following on from that, to prove how difficult it is to perform like a world-beater every day of the week, Trueman proceeded to go right through the First Test to claim just one wicket in each innings.

The appointed place for the Test was Christchurch, a ground where Trueman would reach another more memorable landmark on his next visit, and the pattern of the game was far simpler and easier than any experienced in Australia. The first Test victory of the tour was achieved and the margin was a comfortable innings and 99 runs. England batted first to total 374, but not before seeing the now customary failure by the openers. Ted Dexter filled the breach on this occasion, hitting his maiden Test century, 141, and with Trueman added 81 for the eighth wicket, the latter's share being 21.

Once New Zealand began to bat, the game was safe for England—Tony Lock saw to that. The batsmen were always in trouble against him and he finished with match figures of 11 for 88. The New Zealanders' first innings crumbled steadily until they were tottering on the brink at 102 for 9. At this juncture K. W. Hough strode to the crease and fireworks, New Zealand-style, began to fly in a most remarkable manner. Throughout his career it is doubtful if Trueman ever received such heavy punishment, in such a short space of time, as he did that day at Christchurch in 1959. In nine deliveries Hough blasted Trueman's bowling for 22 runs, including three fours and a six and altogether scored 31 not out, out of a last-wicket stand of 40. It was remarkable hitting by any standards, but coming from a New Zealand number eleven playing in his first Test could only add insult to injury.

Trueman brought the curtain down on the act and there, with the last wicket of the innings was the one scalp he needed.

E. C. Petrie lbw b Trueman 8

The first century had been raised. It arrived in Trueman's

twenty-fifth Test appearance and had taken him almost seven years since making his debut in 1952. When noting that this was the exact mid-point of his career, time-wise, Trueman's final total of 307 wickets is given added brilliance. Taking the matter purely on averages the first 100 had come at the rate of four per game and here another illuminating point arises. It will be seen, as the story unfolds, that this ratio of wickets to Tests rises steadily with Trueman's more consistent selection and shows beyond all doubt that had Trueman played in all the Tests he should have been picked for, his end total would have reached unbelievable proportions.

To return to the Christchurch Test, New Zealand followed on 232 runs behind. Once again Lock had the batsmen mesmerised and bettered his first innings effort of 5 for 31 by taking 6 for 20. Trueman had to be content with the wicket of opener Harris for 20 runs but it mattered little. The result counted most and New Zealand were hustled out for 133. Hough and Petrie were once more the last pair at the crease though on this occasion the tactics were reversed. Rather than hit the ball out of sight, they delighted the crowd by scampering some of the cheekiest singles ever seen in Test cricket. The general idea seemed to be a simple matter of just touching the ball and running like hell! But the game was already lost and it gave splendid entertainment in another delightful little last-wicket stand.

So to Auckland for the last match of an exacting six-month tour. Due to the weather it was a depressing anti-climax with either side managing to bat only once. Throughout the game a high wind prevailed (there had been a cyclone warning in the area), often blowing off the bails, and it ruined the match as a spectacle from the outset. Reid won the toss for the home side and immediately the New Zealanders were in serious trouble. Half the team were dismissed for 41 in the face of a Trueman who was virtually unplayable. He demonstrated this admirably by opening out with seven successive maidens and at the end of the innings had the excellent figures of 26–12–46–3. Sutcliffe, New Zealand's one world-class batsman, was the only man to bat reasonably in scoring 61 but then Hough arrived at the crease again. A record 18,000 crowd had braved the terrible weather and imminent possibility of a cyclone and Hough made sure they did not go away disappointed.

This time it was Tyson who was the victim of Hough's savage onslaught. Five boundaries zoomed from his bat in two overs as he hit up 24 not out to boost a sagging New Zealand total to 181 and in the process scored all the runs in the last wicket partnership. By some strange quirk these two Tests against England were the only appearances Hough made for his country and they gave him the enviable Test Match average of 62! In three innings, for once out, he lashed 62 furious runs against two of the fastest bowlers in the world and then never played for New Zealand again. For an unheard-of number eleven New Zealand batsman, who was really a bowler, that was quite some performance.

When England batted, May was in outstanding form, scoring 124 not out. With Trueman, he added 50 in an unbroken eighth wicket stand but with the score at 311 for 7 the match came to an abrupt end. The last two days were completely washed out by rain and the tour was concluded with a rather damp, disappointing draw. All that remained was the long journey home, a short rest and it would be time to start all over again with a five-match series against India.

The whole tour had been very disappointing for a number of unconnected reasons. Far too many players had suffered injuries for an effective combination to be selected that could play together for any length of time and with this unsettled air about the team chances of success were always slim. Five players failed to complete the trip (Statham, Loader, Milton, Bailey and Laker) while several others had lengthy spells on the sidelines. These included Watson, Evans and Subba Row and it came as no great surprise when Dexter was sent for as an emergency replacement halfway through the tour.

The perennial question of doubtful umpiring standards also arose, especially around McInnes in Australia. On Hutton's tour of 1954–5 he had gained a high reputation but during May's campaign he seemed to be involved in every controversy that occurred. More important, was the concrete evidence of a growing problem in world cricket that was also on view in Australia, namely throwing. Australia had several bowlers with highly questionable bowling actions, not least being Meckiff and Rorke and in the next few years this contentious subject was to gain prominence in nearly every cricketing country. Australia, West Indies, South Africa and England all had suspect bowlers but this was only the beginning of the affair. The culmination was to come in 1960 when South Africa toured England. Even then, when the South African Geoff Griffin was no-balled out of Test cricket, the storm did not die away but continued to rumble on for many years and until the rules were made more specific this would always be the case.

Meanwhile, England had to return home and begin picking up the pieces after their disastrous Antipodean enterprise. Fortunately, rebuilding the team was not to take as long as might have been originally envisaged for, already, England had embarked on their most successful period in the history of the game, starting with the two Tests against New Zealand. India came next, followed by a tour to the West Indies, and a home series with South Africa in 1960. Defeat was to be conspicuously absent and was not encountered in a single Test in any of these series. In fact, it was to be June 1961 before England would be beaten again, a run extruding over eighteen consecutive Test Matches stretching back as far as February 1959, some twenty-eight months in all. Significantly, Trueman was an ever-present member of the team through this period.

AVERAGES FOR 1958–9 SERIES *v* NEW ZEALAND: Two Tests, Played Two

Overs	*Mdns*	*Runs*	*Wkts*	*Ave*
44.5	17	105	5	21.00

Inns	*NO*	*Runs*	*HS*	*Ave*
2	1	42	21*	42.00

Catches=4

Match results=New Zealand 0, England 1, 1 Match drawn.

Statistics
1 Total Test wickets=104
2 Total catches=27
3 Total runs=340
4 Total appearances=26

7 India, at home, 1959

After the humiliations suffered at the hands of Australia in the previous winter it came as no surprise when the selectors began ringing the changes for the 1959 home series against India. New blood was needed to revitalise the team and the much gentler opposition provided by India afforded England the opportunity to experiment with several hitherto untried players. In comparison to Australia there was a vast difference in the calibre of the Indians which became instantly apparent when studying their respective track records. Australia was already acknowledged as a world-class side, probably the best in the world at that time, but with India the position was much the opposite. While this was their fifth visit to England, they were still seeking their first Test victory there.

Only once, out of a total of nineteen previous encounters at home and abroad, had a result gone India's way. That had occurred on England's tour to the sub-continent in the winter of 1951–2 but it was very much a 'reserve' team that made the trip. What happened when the Indians faced a full compliment of English Test players has already been described in Chapter Two and the one question uppermost in the minds of everybody concerned with the 1959 series was whether or not the Indians had learnt anything positive from their misfortunes seven years earlier. The answer was emphatically negative.

From the moment the tour began the problems facing the tourists were manifold. The party of seventeen players arrived in early April under the captaincy of D. K. Gaekwad and fine player though he was it was not a happy tour for him. Although he missed only one Test it was obvious from halfway through the summer that he was not in the best of health. In many games he adopted a purely defensive attitude (the not uncommon maxim that 'if we can't win we won't lose') and it was noticeable that when vice-captain Roy took charge the Indians tended to perform much better. Another player who was never really fit was Manjrekar, India's most prolific run-scorer for years, and this was a big blow to the tourists. A batsman of world stature, he never let his side down but his appearance in the Second Test at Lord's was his last of the summer. Following that game he went into hospital for the removal of a knee cap which clearly shows the handicap under which he had been playing.

As a direct result of Manjrekar's enforced absence A. A. Baig was invited to join the team in mid-July. Then only twenty years of age he was studying at Oxford University and his experience of first-class cricket was extremely limited but the move was, nevertheless, an unqualified success. Baig hit centuries in his first two games (102 *v* Middlesex and 112 *v* England) and in doing so, joined the select band of cricketers who have scored a century on their debut in Test Match cricket. In a disappointing summer for the Indians, Baig's brilliance with the bat provided one of the all too rare bright spots amid months of gloom.

When the New Zealanders returned home after their 1958 tour of England there were very few people who thought a Test team from any country could, in the future, perform with less effectiveness than the example set by the New Zealanders. Within the space of twelve months the pundits had been proved wrong. The two teams played exactly the same number of first-class matches, 35, and achieved the same number of wins, 7, but while the New Zealanders suffered only 6 defeats the Indians dismal failings amounted to 11. Their excuses were few and far between. Not even the weather could be blamed, as had been the case to a certain extent with the New Zealanders. On their tour the summer had been appalling but in 1959 the Indians were blessed with the finest weather for a good many years. Taking everything into account, they were lacking in every department. Before being in a position to cope with the world's best their minimum requirements were top-class opening batsmen and at least one genuine pace bowler. As it was, in 1959, they had neither and this deficiency brought an unprecedented string of victories for England.

Trent Bridge was the venue for the First Test and the changes the selectors were determined upon were evident from the very beginning of the series. Three new players were introduced to Test cricket while only six remained from the party which toured Australia. Taylor, Horton and Greenhough were the debutees while May, Cowdrey, Milton, Evans, Trueman and Statham retained their places. May won the toss, so maintaining a remarkable success rate in this fifty-fifty gamble of 66 per cent and his decision to bat was a foregone conclusion. The one innings was sufficient to suit England's needs and apart from one or two early scares were always in command, eventually finishing the match with a day to spare, winning by an innings and 59 runs.

In the early stages England could well have been in trouble. The scoreboard showed 60 for 3 wickets at one time but a century from May soon altered the position and he set the example for the later batsmen to follow. All of the middle order batsmen scored well with half centuries coming from Horton, Barrington and Evans and even the bowlers got in on the act. Statham, 29 not out, and Trueman, 28, added important extra runs to take the final score to 422 all out and the scene was set for a comfortable victory.

England batted one hour into the second day's play and when the Indians began their first innings May used his three fast bowlers (Trueman, Statham and Moss) in carefully planned short, quick-fire bursts. This may have accounted for the snail's-pace scoring rate but whatever the cause the pace of the batting was painstakingly slow. This can be judged from the tea-time score of 79 for 1, made in a little less than three hours. Trueman came out after the break well refreshed and instantly put a different aspect on the game. In two overs he bowled both Umrigar and Roy to have the Indians struggling but Manjrekar remained firm and offered solid resistance until bad light followed by a rainstorm finished play early for the day with the tourists' score standing at 116 for 3.

On the third day the same trio of pace bowlers had the stage to themselves. Apart from five overs bowled by Greenhough, Trueman and company bowled from start of play until the Indians were all out at 2.45 pm. It was a quite inept display of batting, showing once again that the Indians did not have the necessary technique required to play genuine fast bowling. The only players who could be excused were Borde and Nadkarni, both of whom were suffering from injuries but, on a hard, true pitch little could be said for the remainder. Borde had a finger broken playing a delivery from Trueman while Nadkarni had severely damaged his hand when attempting to catch Statham during the England first innings but these were the exceptions. The rest of the team could not face up to the speed of England's three front-line bowlers and with Trueman always looking dangerous the innings closed at 206, his share of the spoils amounting to a well-controlled analysis of 24–9–45–4.

May did not hesitate to enforce the follow-on. The deficit to make up was 216 and in the remaining time on the third day India advanced to 96 for 3. Over the weekend there was a fair amount of heavy rain and when play resumed on the Monday the crowd was very sparse. Statham took over the mantle of chief wicket-taker on this fourth day to have the match concluded by 3.30 pm and he finished with the fine figures of 5 for 31 to his name. Trueman took a back seat to claim 2 for 44 but the Indians were still routed. The final total of 157 was well short of the total required to make England bat again and, on a day when Statham was at his best, it was a pity that only something like 500 people were present to witness his fine bowling.

In keeping with tradition, Lord's staged the Second Test. England went one better than at Trent Bridge in that they completed their task with consummate ease before close of play on the third day, one day sooner than in the First Test. Roy took charge of the Indian team in place of the injured Gaekwad but his solitary success on the first day was in winning the toss. It was not pace that upset the tourists on this occasion but the spin of Greenhough who claimed five wickets in the modest first innings total of 168 all out made by India. Their last six wickets crashed for a paltry 20 runs and the batting was failing to stand up against any type of bowling, whether fast or slow, but the Indians hit back before close of play to snatch three English wickets for 50 runs. They were not quite on top but there was room for optimism if the Indians could continue the good work on the morrow.

This they did in splendid fashion and it was one of the rare occasions in the whole series when the visitors were well in command of the situation. Three more were quickly snapped up on the second morning, putting England in considerable trouble at 80 for 6 but help was near at hand. Barrington, receiving very good support from the tail, was the hero of the hour. First with Trueman, he helped to add 20 to the score and then came the highlight, an excellent stand of 84 with Statham which helped to swing the game England's way. It gave their side the lead and another last wicket partnership of 42 stretched this to 58. Barrington was last out, for 80, having accomplished a fie task in putting England slightly on top overall.

Trueman reiterated England's claim to superiority in typical fashion in hi very first over. It was shades of 1952 all over again with India 0 for 2 and the now more restrained Trueman on yet another Test hat-trick. In 1952 he had been a wild, tearaway, ferocious bowler. Seven years later he had matured into a cultured, controlled bowler with rare attributes of electrifying shock speed allied with subtle change of pace. Coupled with his ability to move the ball either way, Trueman was now a far more dangerous bowler than in the early days when he relied on sheer speed, and while the speed was still evident, this now fully matured articte was an infinitely better bowler. Roy was the first to fall victim to Trueman in India's second innings. May took the catch at third slip and Horton collected the second one off Umrigar, surely one of Trueman's most welcome adversaries, only a few yards further away in the gully.

As always, the hat-trick did not materialise. Nor did any more wickets in the innings but the first two had put India well on the way to defeat. At 42 for 4 a complete collapse appeared imminent but Manjrekar, the one Indian batsman to bat consistently well against Trueman, and Kirpal Singh averted this with a stand of 89. They scored 61 and 41 respectively but once they were parted the end was in sight for India. Their total reached 165 leaving England the comparatively simple task of scoring 108 for victory. On the bowling front the wickets were spread evenly among four, Moss and Greenhough claiming two each and Statham three in addition to Trueman's brace.

The target appeared to present England with no more than a gentle practce session to accumulate the runs. However, when both openers fell with only 12 runs on the board an exciting, perhaps even surprising finish, became a possibility. Not that May and Cowdrey had any such thoughts. They put paid to the notion and tore into the Indian bowling with such effect that only seventy minutes were required to hit the remaining 96 runs still outstanding. It was a comfortable eight-wicket victory, while for Trueman it was one of his quieter Test Matches, with three wickets to his name but his shattering burst at the beginning of the second innings showed he still possessed all the qualities needed for hostile fast bowling.

The series continued at Headingley, where Peter May equalled the world record, held by Frank Wooley, of fifty-two consecutive Test appearances. Unfortunately, because of illness he was unable to play in the next Test and thus missed taking the record for himself. Of all the captains Trueman played under for England, May was probably the best. Hutton was undoubtedly a better batsman but May had special qualities which enabled him to be a true leader of men. Many were the times when he had to go to the wicket with England in dire straits and the numerous occasions on which he rescued his team was the prime way to give encouragement to other players, namely by personal example. It not only gave a lead for other players to follow but also gained their respect, a trait every captain must have and May had it in abundance from the men he was chosen to lead. As well as being a very fine captain, May was also one of the most exciting, attacking players in the world in his day and easily England's best. When he retired from the game in 1962 it was a sad day for English cricket and many, not least the author, thought it was at least five years too soon. Players of his calibre, temperament and class are rare jewels among many brightly glinting stones that metaphorically turn into cricketers.

For the Headingley game England continued its policy of introducing new players. Pullar and Rhodes were the latest new recruits to join the ranks and their inexperience had little bearing on the result, quite the reverse, and England again triumphed with more than two days to spare. Gaekwad returned for the tourists, having recovered from injury, and began by winning the toss. The pitch was ideal for batting. It lacked pace or lift and by batting first the tourists should have capitalised on the conditions to build a decent, if not large, total. It was not to be. In keeping with their usual form that summer the batsmen failed completely. In less than a day's play they were bundled out for 161, putting England well on the way to victory by close of play on that same first day.

Trueman bowled a mere five overs in his first spell. There was nothing in the pitch for him to utilise and the conditions were as near to anything the Indians would encounter in England that would resemble the pitches of their homeland. Rhodes replaced Trueman after his first spell to make a most dramatic entry into Test cricket. Two wickets in his first two overs rocked the Indian boat dangerously close to a sinking position. It was not until Umrigar joined Gaekwad at 23 for 4 that any resistance was shown to the English bowling and a stand of 52 helped to retrieve some lost ground for India but the recovery was only temporary. The innings closed at 161, with Nadkarni and Tamhane the only other batsmen to make any impression and it was mainly due to their efforts that the last four wickets added 86 runs. The fast bowlers had once again dominated the batting completely, with all three returning excellent figures: Rhodes 18.4–3–50–4, Trueman 15–6–30–3 and Moss 22–11–30–2. In the time remaining on the first day England's openers reduced the arrears by some 51 runs.

The second day saw the first wicket partnership continue to flourish until Pullar was brilliantly caught at square-leg by Borde. The stand, worth 146, was England's best such effort for some twenty-six Tests, ending a depressing run of failures by the openers, and Pullar's share was a highly satisfactory 75. India claimed two more wickets as England advanced to 183 for 3 but there their powers of penetration ceased for a considerable length of time. Cowdrey and Barrington joined forces in a stand worth 193 runs which was not ended until the latter fell to Nadkarni for 80. At the close England were 408 for 8 with Cowdrey still there on 148. May's position was so strong that he could have declared there and then had he so wished but he decided otherwise.

In very hot weather on the third morning England continued in unrelenting manner. The runs came in even time and at 483 for 8 May called a halt with Cowdrey still not out, having achieved his highest Test score up to that stage of his career, the innings realising some 160 runs. The declaration set India a daunting task. Requiring 322 runs to avoid an innings defeat they had to decide upon one of two courses open to them. Either they could go for the runs and attempt to set England a target or they could try the unlikely ploy of batting the better part of three days and thereby force a draw. Both tasks were utterly beyond their wildest dreams.

Trouble arose right at the start of the innings with Moss removing Apte. The bowler was then forced to leave the field with a strained back but Trueman took over where Moss left off and began a fine, spirited spell of bowling. Roy and Ghorpade were his victims to put the Indians in serious trouble at 38 for 3. At this point some stout resistance began between Borde, who made 41, and Umrigar, with 39, and together the pair added 69 to the score but once they were parted the inevitable collapse began. The last six wickets crashed for the addition of a scant 42 to give England an impressive victory by an innings and 173 runs. The Indian second innings was completed shortly before 5 pm and in scoring 149 the whole affair lasted a shade less than three hours. Only once in six innings to date in the series had the tourists succeeded in scoring more than 200 runs but on this occasion at Headingley it was not the terrors of Trueman or other fast bowlers who had brought about their downfall.

It had become obvious late on the Friday evening, the second day's play, that there were one or two spots on the wicket and the ball was beginning to turn sharply. Consequently, after Trueman and Moss had made the all-important initial break-through Close and Mortimore stepped into the fray. Both howled their off-breaks with commendable skill and accuracy to round off the innings with some very good figures, Close 4 for 35 and Mortimore 3 for 35. It appeared that the Indians were under an hypnotic influence no matter what speed the ball was bowled at them. Whether fast or slow, it made no difference. They still collapsed.

The Fourth Test, played at Old Trafford, saw England continue in a winning vein but this was by far the best game of the series and the only one to go into the fifth day. India brought in their replacement batsman Baig for his first Test while

England recalled Mike Smith, Dexter and Illingworth. Originally, Cowdrey was one of the players omitted from the side but when Peter May was taken ill shortly before the game he was brought back into the team and was captain of England for the first time in his career. The Manchester match was Trueman's thirtieth appearance for his country in seven years, yet in that time he had played under just three different captains: Hutton, May and now Cowdrey.

The illness was untimely for May, just one match short of the world record number of consecutive Test appearances but there was no doubting its seriousness. He watched the first two days' play before going into hospital for an operation and any further active participation in the series was out of the question. How much this illness contributed to his future poor form on the winter tour of West Indies is difficult to assess. However, as the wound reopened during the tour, necessitating him to fly home for further treatment, it is plain to see that it was a troublesome complaint and illness of this sort was to be with May for the rest of his career.

Cowdrey commenced his new appointment with a minor success by winning the toss. The obvious choice was to bat first yet early in the innings England might possibly have run into trouble. In the stifling, overbearing conditions the Indian medium-pace bowlers were able to make the ball swing considerably. It was a home from home in such sun-drenched weather but the Indians failed to make the most of their chances. Five possible catches were offered in the morning session in all of which only one was accepted. This solitary wicket brought Pullar and Cowdrey together and in a stand of 131 they set the tone for the rest of the innings. Pullar himself went on to score 131, registering his maiden Test century, as also did Smith in scoring exactly 100 and the England innings ended at the sizeable total of 490. In view of India's previous poor batting form there appeared to be little to prevent England going four-up in the series.

When India began batting on the second afternoon play followed a similar pattern to previous games. Rhodes was the most troublesome bowler for them and at close of play the tourists' score stood at 127 for 6. There was every prospect of

Australia's opening batsman Lawry is brilliantly caught by Trueman off Allen's bowling on the fourth day of the fourth Test at Old Trafford, 1961.

Trueman in devastating form during the first day of the first Test against Australia at Brisbane, 1962. He dismissed Australia's leading batsmen to end the day with figures of three wickets for 62 runs.

Trueman being applauded off the field at Edgbaston after he had taken 12 wickets in the third Test against the West Indies, 1963.

Hunt

Hall

Sobers

The Edgbaston Test: three of Trueman's victims

With this wicket in the final Test at the Oval in 1963 -- that of Lance Gibbs – Trueman broke A.L. Valentine's record of 33 wickets in a Test series.

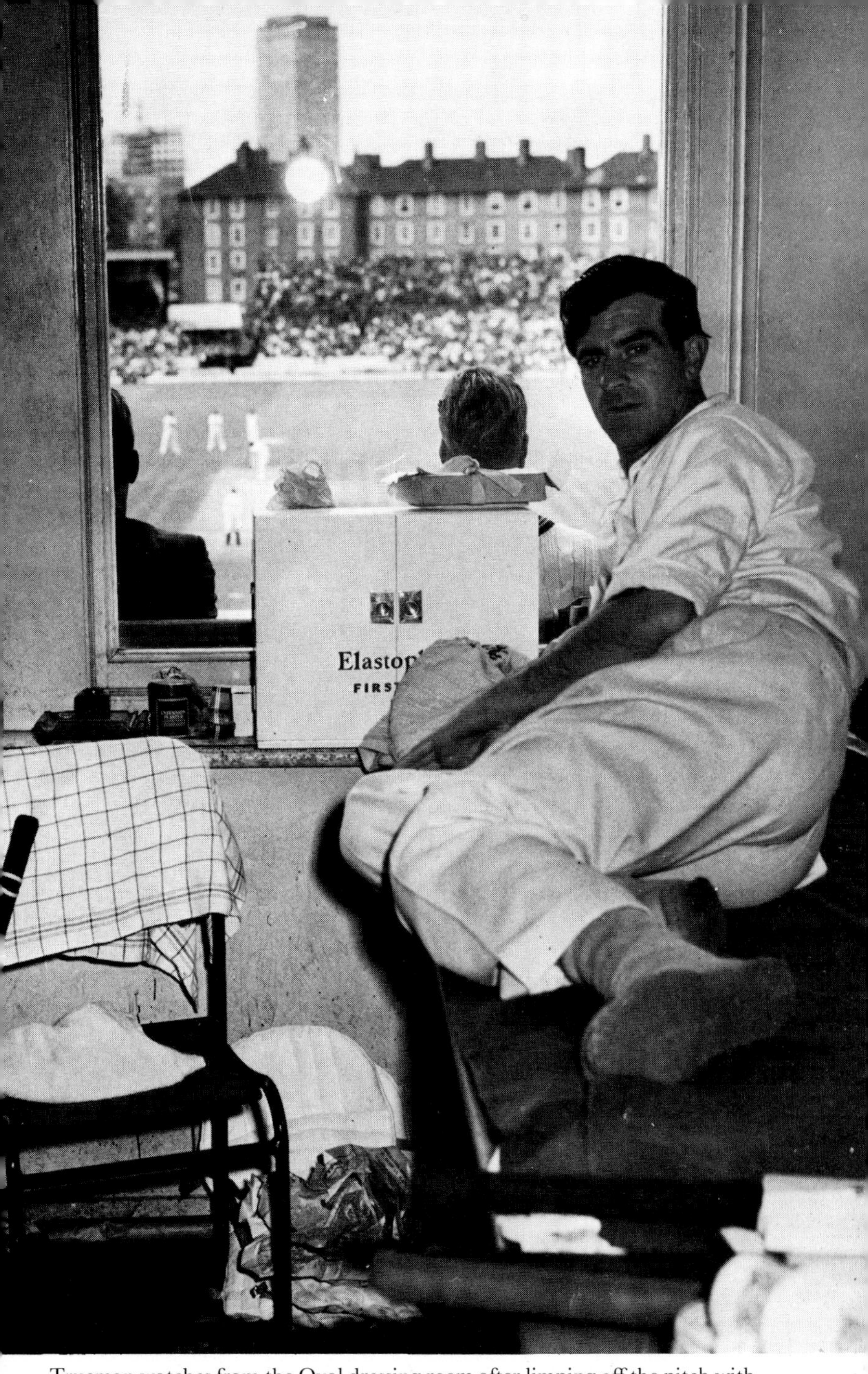

Trueman watches from the Oval dressing room after limping off the pitch with an injured ankle.

Trueman is caught in the slips by Bobby Simpson during the first Test against Australia at Trent Bridge, 1964.

them having to follow on but, before play began on the third day, Cowdrey allayed these fears by announcing he would not ask the Indians to bat again should the choice be open. It was an unusual step to take but the weather was continuing to be nothing less than uninterrupted sunshine and the prospect of three successive Tests being completed in three days did not augur well for future gate receipts especially as Manchester was beginning a holiday week that weekend.

Solely due to a splendid innings of 75 by Borde, his best up to that time in Test cricket, India were able to top 200 for the second time in the series. It was a near thing, the final score being 205 and Borde's effort was the only positive piece of cricket offered by the Indian batsmen. The wickets were evenly distributed amongst the bowlers, Trueman taking 1 for 29 off fifteen overs, but a surprising name on the list was that of Barrington. He played in the same county side, Surrey, as his erstwhile captain May who, although he must have known of his capabilities as a leg-spin bowler, rarely gave Barrington the chance to try his arm in Test Matches. Cowdrey took a different view with the result that Barrington picked up 3 for 36.

England duly took the crease a second time. There were four individual scores over 40 in the total of 265 for 8 but no batsman was able to penetrate the half-century barrier. Regardless of this England had an impregnable lead. It totalled a mammoth 540, an impossible target for any side to achieve in the last innings of a Test, let alone the Indians. That was the unanimous verdict but the Indians did not view matters in the same light. So well did they bat on the fourth day, particularly Baig, that they not only restored their lost pride but at one time were even in with a chance of victory.

Batting with Contractor, Baig lay the foundation of the innings. They put together 109 for the second wicket, by far the best partnership of the series for the tourists and when he lost Contractor for 56, the dapper Baig continued to take the fight to England with the help of Umrigar. When he was 85 Baig was struck a nasty blow on the temple from a ball by Rhodes which forced him to leave the field. He resumed his innings at the fall of Nadkarni's wicket on the last day and while Umrigar and Baig were still together England could not be certain of victory.

The nervous nineties affected the young Indian but finally, after spending half an hour on 96, Baig swept Rhodes to the boundary to complete his maiden Test century. It was the third such achievement in the match and easily the most appreciated by both the players and crowd alike.

Of more serious concern to England was the steadily mounting score. Both Baig and Umrigar were going extremely well, stealing quick singles and generally looking well in command of the situation. However remote, victory was a possibility for the Indians while the pair remained in harness but when he was 112 Baig's innings was brought to an end in brilliant fashion by Dexter. The batsmen pulled very hard at a ball from Mortimore and set off for a run immediately. Baig thought the ball was past Dexter but he picked the ball up and threw in to Swetman in the twinkling of an eye. By the time Baig turned to recover his ground he was hopelessly stranded and an innings lasting four hours twenty minutes was summarily brought to a rather sad conclusion though it was a marvellous reflex action on Dexter's part.

Only Umrigar stood between England and victory now. Baig had seen the score rise from 44 for 1 to 321 for 6 but his departure was the end of India's hopes and once Umrigar reached his first Test century in England he realised there was not enough batting strength left on the challenge. He took his score on to 118 before falling and then Trueman stepped in to finalise proceedings. First he caught Surendranath and shortly after bowled Gupte. With three-and-three-quarter hours to spare England were home, victors by 171 runs. On the credit side for the Indians was their total of 376, their highest of the series, which showed that they could, at times, stand up successfully against England's battery of fast bowlers.

Trueman's contribution to the game was more workmanlike than spectacular. Brilliant displays were impossible in every match and, similar to Lord's, he took only three wickets in what was another quiet game by his own standards. The trio at Old Trafford took his total for the series to 17 and there lies the answer to his overall performances. No matter how subdued he appeared to be he was still England's leading wicket-taker to date in the series, well ahead of his nearest rival, and it showed how much more consistency was his stamp now rather than dramatic, spectacular one-match successes.

At the Oval in the Fifth Test England were facing a tantalising prospect for the second time in the space of a year. Up to this point in the series England had drawn an exact parallel with the 1958 rubber against New Zealand by winning all of the first four Tests. It provided a second chance to make a clean sweep of all five Tests in a series for the first time in history and where they had failed in 1958 there were no such mistakes against the Indians. The match was over before lunch on the fourth day with England easy winners by an innings and 27 runs. Thus history was made and a five-nil victory was accomplished. Only twice before, both times by Australia at home, had the feat been achieved and both occasions were some forty to fifty years in the past. The first had been against England in 1920–1 while the second was against South Africa in 1931–2.

The outcome at the Oval was a formality from the end of the Indian first innings. Gaekwad won the toss and on a pitch that was ideal decided to bat. To be dismissed for 140 runs on such favourable conditions was a most inept performance by the tourists but far worse was the length of time spent occupying the crease. In all, the innings lasted five hours, a depressingly long time in which to accumulate so few but as the final total was so low it disproved totally any theory that negative, ponderous batting was the way to counteract the speed of Trueman and Statham.

The architect of the Indians' steady dismissal was Trueman. It was never a collapse because, despite the low score, the batsmen were never hurried out and Contractor provided a prime example. In the time the majority of class batsmen take to score a century (he actually batted three hours twenty minutes) Contractor mustered only 22 runs and it was ironical that two tail-enders should have to show their peers how little venom there was in the wicket. Tamhane and Surendranath staged a defiant eighth wicket stand of 58 but it was no more than a token flurry. Trueman came back to finish off the innings and so completed a praiseworthy spell of bowling which also gave him his best return of the series: 17–6–24–4.

For the first time in several years England's innings opened out with two left-hand batsmen, Geoff Pullar and Ramon Subba Row. Pullar went first, quickly followed by Cowdrey but once Smith teamed up with Subba Row England flourished again. In a record third wicket partnership between the countries the pair added 169 and both got into the nineties but neither could make the magical three-figure mark. Smith fell at 98, Subba Row on 94 and this left the way open for Illingworth and Swetman to stage their version of a record-breaking partnership as they added 102 for the seventh wicket. Both scored half centuries to assist ably in England's final score of 361 all out.

India required 221 to make the home side bat again, a not excessive target but one which, with their obvious limitations, would provide a stern test. This was the case and at one stage of the proceedings the match was in danger of finishing on the third day. Statham set the scene, taking the first two wickets before the score had reached 20. With an hour and twenty minutes left for play the score had risen to 105 for the loss of three more wickets but then Nadkarni and Ghorpade began to defend grimly. They stayed together for an hour when bad light and a thunderstorm ended play for the day with the tourists requiring another 75 runs to avoid an innings defeat.

With five wickets remaining this should have been possible. The overnight batsmen carried their partnership to 53, the highest of the innings, before Ghorpade was bowled by Greenhough but Nadkarni continued to hang on grimly. He eventually fell to Illingworth for what, on paper, looked a good score but four hours to score 76 is rather a long time even when trying to stave off defeat. The end was in sight with Nadkarni's departure and when Trueman returned it became a reality. He took the last two wickets, making three in all in the innings, and in less than an hour and a half's play the last five wickets had fallen for 48 runs. Trueman's analysis of 3 for 30 gave him seven wickets in the match and, similar to his first innings effort, this was also his best match return of the series. The highlight, of course, was that by gaining the victory England had made a clean sweep of a series for the first time in over eighty years of Test cricket, and it was a very fine achievement on the part of all the players concerned.

In many ways, however, the series was a disappointment, notwithstanding England's excellent performance. A margin of five-nil was an outstanding entry to make in any record book but the opposition had made it rather easy for the home side. At best, their batting was fragile while the bowling lacked the penetration necessary when playing against top-class batsmen. For Trueman, it was another relatively quiet period with no really outstanding performances. But his pattern of play was changing discernibly. Now, he was more steady and purposeful with his bowling rather than attempting to blast the opposition out with every ball. The explosive, shattering force that had sent the Indians home shell-shocked in 1952 was not in evidence in 1959 but he was still England's leading wicket-taker with twenty-four victims to his credit. Nonetheless, Trueman was an infinitely better bowler at this stage of his career and he went about his work in a less obtrusive manner picking up wickets regularly rather than claiming vast numbers in only one or two matches. Consistency and thoughtfulness, they were of the essence in this middle part of his career and Trueman was rightly moving towards being one of the foremost fast bowlers in the world as a result of those traits.

What the 1959 series proved was that Trueman had finally arrived as a Test bowler. 1958, against New Zealand, had been too wet for him to get into his stride and the winter tour to Australia had not given him a great deal of scope. That is not to say it was a wasted journey for it did give Trueman valuable experience and against India it was evident that he had learnt a great deal. Variation of pace, much greater accuracy and his tendency to 'think' batsmen out, as against blasting them out, had all become his trademarks. With this natural process of maturing came the awareness that possibly Trueman was destined for far greater things. He could go right to the top but only time would tell if the promise would be fulfilled that had been evident over the previous seven years.

To this end, the outcome was firmly in Trueman's own hands. Since his inclusion for the Third Test on the Australian tour, he had played in ten consecutive Tests, which equalled his previous most consistent period of selection. This was to stretch to twenty-four consecutive appearances before he finally lost his place at the end of the 1961 home series against Australia. Trueman was not the type of bowler to throw away a chance like that. In this period of twenty-four games, he was to take 104 wickets, which more than justified his repeated selection, and they raised his total of Test wickets from 90 to 194. In that time there could be no doubting who was England's premier fast bowler.

For the time being Trueman had to be content with his present total of Test wickets. At the end of the Indian series it stood at 128 with the next item on the agenda a visit to the West Indies in the winter of 1959–60. Much water had passed under the bridge since he was last there, including a home series against West Indies, but bitter memories could take a long time to fade and the outcome was very much in the balance. There was the possibility of upsets occurring but, happily, there were none. This second Caribbean trip would be a far happier tour than the previous one and was certainly far more successful than many people originally anticipated.

AVERAGES FOR 1959 SERIES *v* INDIA: Five Tests, Played Five

Overs	*Mdns*	*Runs*	*Wkts*	*Ave*
177.4	53	401	24	16.70

Inns	*NO*	*Runs*	*HS*	*Ave*
6	0	61	28	10.16

Catches=5

Match results=England 5, India 0.

Statistics
1 Total Test wickets=128
2 Total catches=32
3 Total runs=401
4 Total appearances=31

8 West Indies, on tour, 1959/60

The party chosen to travel to the Caribbean under the captaincy of Peter May for the winter tour of 1959–60 received a considerable amount of adverse criticism from the sporting media. Following the resounding defeat in Australia twelve months previous, MCC picked a 'new look' squad but it was not enough to satisfy the critics. In retrospect, the team was not one of the best ever to leave England but the players still achieved what many thought was an impossibility in that they won a series in the West Indies for the very first time and in doing so confounded the pessimists. In administrative company with May went Walter Robins as manager and the combination proved successful. Unlike the acrimonious affair of 1953–4 this subsequent tour was an altogether more enjoyable affair and with a victory coming in the series as well there could be no complaints from any quarter.

Well though the tour went, it was not all a bed of roses. Several contentious points arose but with common sense, tact and diplomacy they were never allowed to get out of hand. At one stage, when a riot on the third day of the Second Test halted play, there was some discussion of the tour being terminated. Robins, commendably, would not hear of any such suggestion and MCC completed the task they had originally set out to accomplish. Apart from the riot, time-wasting, continual use of the bumper and throwing were the other most controversial issues to arise.

In the Tests May brought field placing into the fine art category. By asking his bowlers to aim a shade outside off-stump to a well-placed field all the leading West Indian batsmen found scoring difficult. They were adventurous, carefree strokemakers by nature and this somewhat negative tactic by May meant the run-rate scarcely moved above 40 per hour throughout the series. There was also a great deal of time lost between the overs or when the field changed over with left and right-hand batsmen at the crease together. This brought the over rate down to a tediously low level but May could claim some justification for his tactics. The aim was to win the series, nothing less, and once the vital first victory had been gained it became a matter of winning again if possible but, by the same token, making absolutely certain they did not lose. A one-nil win in the series was sufficient for England's needs and therefore May, if he wished, could ignore the critics and the end result justified the means by which it was achieved.

On the delicate question of short-pitched bowling, English batsmen faced a veritable barrage of bumpers from Hall and Watson. At times, three and four an over were dispatched at the batsmen, a ridiculously high proportion, but little was done to curb this potentially lethal form of attack. Only at Trinidad, in the Second Test, did the West Indian bowlers receive a warning. Hall and Watson got one apiece from the umpires and it worked the oracle for a short time, especially when Trueman and Statham returned the dose in equal measure when they bowled. After that little was seen of short-pitched bowling for the rest of that match but the problem persisted throughout the series without further remonstrations from the umpires.

In the two or three years prior to this tour throwing had steadily made its presence felt in the game. It was an ever-increasing problem, not just in the West Indies, but all over the world. Because of this it was inevitable that some of their bowlers should come under close scrutiny. Australia, England and to some extent South Africa (though in their case the problem would not present itself for another twelve months) all knew of the intricacies of the problem and as time went by it was becoming more obvious that measures would have to be taken before chaos took over. All told, West Indies had half a dozen bowlers with suspect actions, two of whom actually appeared in Tests. To make matters worse, the situation was not helped when one leading West Indian umpire resigned because he knew he would receive no official support after he made it clear that he intended to call a certain bowler for throwing.

Umpiring in the West Indies is not a task to be undertaken by the faint-hearted. Volatile crowds, plus a combination of drink, gambling and the hot weather make the men in white coats all-too-easy targets for people to vent their anger upon when things are not going right. In an attempt to alleviate some of the problems the authorities adopted a policy previously untried in the West Indies. A panel of umpires was formed who would stand for the five Tests overall, rather than picking two umpires from the island where the individual Tests would be played. Theoretically, the idea was sound in principle but it failed to erase any of the old problems. The men in the middle were understandably reluctant to carry out their duties to the strict letter of the law when they knew they would receive no co-operation whatsoever from the authorities. Hence the resignation of one umpire who was prepared to stand by what he considered to be right.

A final point before dealing with the tour proper, and a very good series indeed for Trueman, arises over the position of Peter May as captain of the side. Prior to the tour commencing there had been some doubt as to his fitness. During the summer of 1959 he had undergone an operation for an internal complaint which caused him to miss quite a lot of first-class cricket, including the last two Tests against India. Undeterred by this setback May declared himself fit enough to participate on the tour. As a player and captain of the highest integrity there can be no reason to surmise he thought otherwise but, sadly, events proved him to be mistaken. Shortly before the Second Test began the wound reopened and the resulting pain and discomfort must have been intense but the captain decided to keep the matter to himself for a considerable time. In many ways this was foolish in the extreme and finally the position became so acute that May had to fly home for further treatment. This left Cowdrey to fill the captain's role and Subba Row took over as vice-captain.

May's stand was certainly courageous both on a personal front and from the point of view of his team but it was hardly wise. The state of his health was the main reason for his poor form with the bat, though he did manage one century against Jamaica. However, when it was bandied about as an underlying cause for a curious incident in the Third Test when May would not allow Kanhai a runner the matter was beginning to get out of hand. If that reasoning were true then the severity of the wound was beginning to affect May's mental faculties and, for a man of his stature, that is a ludicrous suggestion. A more simple and straightforward explanation could well be that May genuinely thought he was entitled to refuse a runner to the batsman under the laws as they stood at that time. Even the umpires were not certain when the incident actually occurred, thus proving how ambiguous the situation was, but when it became clear afterwards that May had been wrong he made an immediate apology to his opposite number, Alexander. For all of his sufferings May never failed as a captain. He retained control, handing the position over to Cowdrey with England holding a one-nil lead and up until the time of his departure May had done everything that was required of him.

With the background to the tour complete the most important ingredient of all remains, the five Tests. Bridgetown was the starting point for the series and England went into the First Test severely restricted in attack due to the loss of Statham through injury. Moss was the chosen deputy, with a place also going to Allen for his first Test appearance. The pitch had a lifeless look about it when May won the toss, the first in an eventual sequence of five, and he took the option of batting first. The decision was sound. Apart from one or two early surprises England were rarely in trouble with Dexter and Barrington paving the way towards a final score of 482 all out. Hall and Watson used the bouncer liberally from the beginning of the innings, extracting a surprising amount of bounce from the dead pitch, but centuries from the two prior-named middle-order batsmen were the perfect reply. Barrington's effort was his first such score in Test cricket while Dexter batted from the fall of the fourth wicket right through the remainder of the innings to remain undefeated on 136.

Over the course of two-and-a-half days in the field there was little cause for pleasure to West Indies followers, with the exception of Alexander's achievement behind the stumps. In addition to being wicket-keeper he was also captain and by dismissing five batsmen, all caught, in the England first innings he set a record for West Indies in Test Matches. The home team's first innings began at lunch-time on the third day and immediately ran into trouble when McMorris was run out in peculiar circumstances, his dismissal coming off a no-ball. By close of play the score amounted to 114 for 3, placing England in a useful position but a stalemate situation was rapidly approaching. A fourth wicket partnership was beginning to develop between Sobers and Worrell which effectively ruled out any possibility of the game ending with a definite result.

The pair joined forces at 4.50 pm on the Friday of the match. Not until 11.40 am on the Tuesday were they parted and in that time 399 runs were added to the score. It was the highest West Indian partnership for any wicket and the highest fourth-wicket stand ever against England, with Sobers hitting 266 and Worrell 197 not out. Throughout their stay at the crease just three chances were offered and as two were relatively simple England could only blame themselves for the partnership flourishing so profusely. Sobers gave a difficult caught and bowled opportunity to Trueman when 7, followed by a much easier offering to Allen at mid-off when 40, while Worrell gave the most straightforward of all three to Illingworth at mid-on when 109. None was caught and West Indies capitalised handsomely.

In terms of time the two batsmen made a banquet, not merely a meal, out of their stay at the crease. Sobers was there ten hours forty-seven minutes, Worrell eleven hours twenty minutes but by the end of the fifth day a draw was inevitable. Trueman ended the marathon by bowling Sobers with the scoreboard on 501 but it brought little chance of a victory to England. The same applied for West Indies. On the final day they failed to push the score along, adding only 77 in two hours ten minutes, and when the declaration came it was meaningless. The time left for play amounted to two hours forty minutes and England faced a deficit on the first innings of 81. Predictably, Pullar and Cowdrey had no difficulty in batting out time.

On Trueman's part, he did not fare at all badly in the West Indies innings. Out of a total of 563 for 8 declared his analysis made commendable reading, 47–15–93–4, and to take half of the wickets to fall while giving away just two runs an over from very nearly fifty overs was very creditable. It certainly gave ample proof to the home side that he was going to be a force to be reckoned with in the months ahead, a somewhat pleasing contrast in comparison to his previous visit in 1953–4.

The Second Test, at Port of Spain, brought about the one decisive result of the series, much to England's joy. Primarily it was Trueman's bowling in the West Indies first innings which made possible the 256 run victory but the occasion had an added significance in that it was the only time in their careers that he and Statham were responsible for the complete demolition of a Test innings. Trueman claimed 5 for 35, his best-ever figures in any of his eight Tests in the Caribbean, and Statham three wickets while there were two run-outs. One of those run-outs was to have disastrous consequences. A full-scale riot immediately developed after the decision was made and play had to be abandoned for the day. A similar event occurred on the 1953–4 tour during the Third Test at Georgetown, a game which Trueman missed, and that also had been precipitated by a run-out decision going against a West Indian batsman.

There was nothing to suggest any of the troubles that lay ahead when May won the toss. For the first half-hour Hall and Watson appeared to be getting very little response out of the pitch until they switched ends. A continuous stream of bumpers were hurled at the batsmen and England plunged headlong into trouble. In a rapid succession of dismissals the score slumped to 57 for 3 before Dexter and Barrington set about recovering some lost ground. In two hours thirty-seven minutes 142 runs were added and Barrington went on to score his second century, 121, of the series. At the close of play on the first day England stood at 220 for 4. By courtesy of another century, this time from Mike Smith, the score progressed to 382 before the innings closed near the end of the second day and England could feel at least satisfied with the outcome.

On the first day of the match Hall had received a warning from the umpire for his excessive use of the bouncer. On the second day it was Watson's turn to be similarly spoken to and these verbal asides may well have worked the oracle for there were very few short-pitched deliveries during the rest of the match but not before Trueman and Statham had the last word. Only twenty-six minutes remained for play on the second day when West Indies began to bat for the first time and Hunte and Soloman were greeted with much the same treatment as Hall and Watson had meted out to England's batsmen. Fortunately, that reply by England's opening bowlers brought the matter to a close, for this particular match, though the vexing problem was to arise on several other occasions in the course of the series.

The third day saw a rapid transformation in the fortunes of the two teams and because of a riot that became so fierce play had to be abandoned for the rest of the day. In the face of some deadly accurate fast bowling by Trueman and Statham West Indies collapsed dramatically. Wickets fell with alarming regularity until, with the score at 98 for 8, play was abruptly halted by the riot. It occurred when the eighth wicket fell. Charran Singh, a local player playing in his first Test, was run out for nought and seconds later hundreds of bottles were raining down on the pitch. Within minutes the fracas had escalated into a full-scale battle between rioters and the police and there was no alternative but for the players to seek safety in the dressing-rooms. Several factors lay behind the disgraceful scenes, not least being a combination of heavy drinking and gambling and when Singh was run out it is probable that many people stood to lose a great deal of money as a result.

At Georgetown, in 1953, McWatt had been nearing his century when he was run out and a riot ensued and a similar reasoning can be applied for that occurrence but, sadly, politics, no matter how foreign to cricket, can never be ruled out of the question. This is probably more true of countries such as India and Pakistan but whenever and wherever a riot occurs on a cricket ground agitators are in a position to make political capital out of the proceedings. The net result of the Port of Spain debacle was that play was suspended for the remainder of the third day. However, a greatly relaxed atmosphere prevailed over the last three days and the match finished without further incident.

Aided by Trueman's outstanding bowling of 21–11–35–5 England speedily concluded West Indies' innings on the fourth day. Their total of 112 gave May the opportunity of enforcing the follow-on but rather than adopt a policy of all-out attack he decided upon consolidating the advantage England had gained and the bowlers were given a well-earned rest. As a result, May was able to set West Indies the task of scoring a colossal 501 to win in ten hours. Such a total had never been scored previously by a side batting fourth to win a Test Match and it was not surprising that West Indies attempted to bat out time for a draw.

At close of play on the fifth day West Indies had cause for some optimism that their objective would be reached. A scoreline reading 134 for 2 meant that England still had a deal of good batting to erase before claiming victory but when the wickets of Worrell and Sobers were snapped up early on the sixth morning victory became a distinct possibility. Kanhai alone withstood the England attack. He batted six hours eighteen minutes for 110 but his labours were the singular example of prolonged resistance from West Indies during the last day. The last three wickets crumbled at the same score, 224, and with one hour fifty minutes remaining for play England had clinched a noteworthy success in one of the most dramatic Tests ever to be played at Port of Spain.

Trueman could not repeat his wicket-taking success of the first innings but his overall figures were by no means disappointing, 19–9–44–1. He had played a significant role in the initial breakthrough for England and after two Tests a clear picture was forming concerning Trueman's standard of bowling. Unlike his returns in the Tests on the previous tour he was achieving far greater success. This was a vastly improved Trueman, who was probably at the peak of his career and he would stay there for the next two or three years. As well as taking wickets regularly, ten in the series to date, Trueman was displaying an accuracy that was quite outstanding when considering he was bowling on the run-laden wickets of the West Indies. His average runs per over were within hundredths of a fraction of being exactly two per over and an economy such as that in the Caribbean was nothing short of being brilliant. Now, seven years after his debut, could it be said that the near-perfect fast bowling machine was complete? Speed, control of pace, careful use of the bouncer, consistency and accuracy were all being combined in complete unison and the result was as good a fast bowler as anybody would see throughout the cricketing world.

Sabina Park (so tiny as to be like an atoll in the Pacific when compared with such grounds as Melbourne and Sydney) was the venue for the Third Test. This was to be May's last Test of the tour and shortly after the game he left the party to return to England for treatment to his recurring stomach ailment. For the third time May won the toss and took the almost inevitable decision to bat first on a pitch that resembled polished marble. Over the first day England laboured to 165 for 6, not the best of starts to be made in a Test, but while the scoring rate was slow the cricket was riveting to behold with two splendid individual performances coming from Hall and Cowdrey. The latter batted all day for England and was solely responsible for holding the innings together while Hall could look back on his day's exertions with equal satisfaction; his return was a superb 5 wickets for 35 runs.

On the second day England played resolutely to stage a minor recovery, the last four wickets adding another 112 runs to the total. This effort was made to look more impressive because the last three wickets were responsible for adding 107 runs with Cowdrey again the mainstay of this latter-part of the innings. In partnership with Trueman he added 45 for the eighth wicket and when finally dismissed had put together a well-disciplined, thoughtful 114 runs that were priceless to England's purpose. On the other side of the fence, Hall had career-best figures of 7 for 69, figures that appear slightly distorted after his supreme first-day effort but a brilliant piece of sustained fast bowling all the same.

West Indies commenced their first innings to hold a slight advantage at the end of the second day and this position improved steadily and substantially as the third day progressed. Overnight, between the second and third days, West Indies' score stood at 81 for 2. Throughout the whole of the third day England toiled away without taking a solitary wicket and at the close the home side had edged in front by 14 runs. There was a steady accumulation of runs all day. Sobers was the main instigator of this after being dropped off the bowling of Statham when 2 and he eventually scored 147 before falling lbw to Trueman on the fourth morning. At the start of the fourth day West Indies were well on top but in the one-and-a-half hour session preceding lunch they could only muster 38 runs. Before a record crowd it was a disappointing performance and after the lunch break, when chasing quick runs, the innings folded in startling style. Three wickets fell at the lunch score, 329, from which a recovery was never likely. In all, the last seven wickets fell for the addition of 24 runs to give West Indies a marginal lead of 76. After being so strongly placed it was a poor finale to the innings for West Indies to total only 353 and May's men had shown spirited resolve to battle on tenaciously and keep a grip on the game.

Trueman toiled long and hard through the innings to claim scant reward. His final return was 2 for 82 off thirty-three overs, but he was still maintaining his accuracy with a good deal less than 3 an over coming off his bowling. With England's remaining bowlers performing creditably to conclude rapidly the West Indies' innings the game was evenly poised, after fluctuations in the fortunes of both sides and when Pullar and Cowdrey resumed the challenge in England's second innings this up and down state of affairs continued.

The deficit England faced, 76, proved to be of so little consequence to the openers that they not only reached it but advanced the score over 100 runs ahead of it before both fell at the same total, 177. Cowdrey was once again in particularly good form. In both innings he was showing his true class but fell just 3 runs short of the rare distinction of scoring a century in each innings of a Test Match. While it was an effort worthy of a century fairy tales do not come to pass in the hard realities of Test cricket but, nonetheless, his 97 runs placed England in a relatively strong position. However, in a game of endless changes in the balance of power West Indies were to hit back strongly.

When play was concluded at the end of the fifth day England had slumped to 280 for 9. Cracks began appearing in several places in the wicket and with this wear and tear to exploit West Indies bowlers were able to make the ball shoot and turn unpredictably. Of the recognised batsmen only May batted with any authority but the position was far from good. The lead amounted to just 204 runs and with a full day's play remaining West Indies had a better than ever chance of squaring the series, especially as there was only one English wicket left to account for on the last morning. Allen and Statham were the not-out overnight batsmen and they did England an invaluable service by holding on to the last wicket for forty-five minutes on the sixth morning. Twenty-five runs were added in this time to leave West Indies a final target of 230 in four hours five minutes and in the final reckoning the precious minutes used up by Allen and Statham were to have an important bearing on the result of the match.

Hunte took up the challenge from the first over as West Indies began the chase for runs. He hit 40 in an hour, out of 48, but tragedy came for the home side when Sobers was run out. This curtailed the scoring-rate considerably and at the tea interval the required score had risen to 115 in ninety minutes which was extremely high by Test Match standards. Seldom is a rate of a run a minute achieved in Tests except in short bursts. When a prolonged bout of free scoring is called for it is always much harder to sustain and when Kanhai was bowled by Trueman for 57 West Indies conceded the challenge. They had little alternative with six wickets down and some forty-five minutes remaining for play. To have continued with an attacking policy, with the risks that are inevitably attached could well have presented England with a golden opportunity of going two up in the series. In the event West Indies calmly batted out time to reach 175 for 6 and in the course of the innings Trueman gained another extremely good analysis to finish with figures of 18–4–54–4.

The game had been one of the most exciting of the series. There had been numerous changes in the relative superior positions of the two teams and on the final day the result could have gone either way. The decisive factor came for England at that point with the defiant last-wicket stand by Allen and Statham. The partnership served a dual purpose in that in addition to taking away valuable time from West Indies the runs added made the final target all the more difficult when the home side could eventually begin batting. If the last wicket had fallen early on the last day West Indies would have required a shade more than 200 runs in the better part of five hours and that was a much simpler proposition than the actual target of 230 in five minutes over four hours. The wicket was breaking up, as Trueman readily demonstrated to great effect with his bowling, and the chase always appeared beyond the scope of the West Indies' batsmen and at the end a draw was perhaps the fairest result to a very exciting, well-fought contest.

Towards the end of the last day a disconcerting incident occurred when May refused Kanhai the services of a runner. The batsman was suffering from cramp and in the discussion which followed it appeared that neither the captains nor the umpires knew the exact legality of the situation. On the face of it, it did appear to be a somewhat unsporting gesture on May's part but he probably thought he was acting within his rights as the laws stood at that time. The matter was resolved when he apologised to Alexander but it did tend to overshadow a most sporting game.

For reasons already outlined, May took no further part in the series. Cowdrey assumed command in the field and England's one-nil lead in the series necessarily dictated his approach to the remaining two Tests. As a result of the Sabina Park game the onus had to be on West Indies to attack if they were to salvage anything from the series but it was also very evident that only under exceptional circumstances would England succeed in winning again in either of the last two Tests. Caution, therefore, had to be the watchword.

This became apparent at Georgetown in the Fourth Test where Cowdrey continued England's good luck with the toss but a desperately slow pace was seen when England batted. In the five hours' play on the first day the four men who occupied the crease could muster only 152 runs and a determination not to lose was becoming the overriding ambition rather than make any attempt at winning. The crawl continued on the second day until an hour from the close when the final English wicket fell with the score at 295 but, painfully slow as England's batting had been, worse was to follow. The third day saw West Indies add a paltry 107 runs to the score and even the loss of forty minutes' play because of rain could not be attributed to such a poor effort. There was no doubt that the bowling and Cowdrey's field placings were defensive but not once was an attempt made to force the pace by the batsmen.

West Indies eventually declared on the fifth day at 402 for 8, a lead of 107, and with eight hours remaining in all for play the home side's only hope of forcing a result was to bowl England out for a reasonable score. On such a placid pitch this was never remotely possible. The pitch became more and more lifeless as the English second innings progressed; at the end of the fifth day the score stood at 110 for 2. The benign nature of the wicket was then highlighted on the last day when West Indies failed to take a single wicket until half an hour from the close of play. A draw was inevitable, and had been virtually from the first day, and when stumps were drawn to conclude the game England had aimlessly batted out time to reach 344 for 8.

This made for the second occasion in the series on which West Indies had batted only once over the full six days of a Test. In view of this limitation in the number of opportunities Trueman had at bowling at the opposition, he was doing very well to be leading the bowling. Furthermore, he was en route to claiming a record number of wickets by an English bowler on a West Indian tour and to achieve it from eight, as against a possible ten innings, was further evidence of Trueman's splendid consistency and control. Out of the Fourth Test he gleaned 3 for 116 off forty overs. It was scant reward for a long session of hard labour but once again the average runs per over did not creep above three and this fine standard of accuracy was to remain throughout the series.

The climax of four months in the Caribbean came when the teams returned to Port of Spain for the Fifth Test. England's hard-pressed cricketers faced an extra problem for this match when, in the wake of May's departure, Statham was also forced to return home. His son lay dangerously ill in hospital and the only sensible thing for MCC and Statham to do was make the speediest arrangements possible for him to fly back to England. With such a distressing problem on his mind it would have been impossible for Statham to have completed the tour and give of his best at the same time. The dilemma placed him in an intolerable situation and the wisest course of action was quite rightly taken. In a sad way, the event provided an unexpected bonus for Trueman. In the absence of Statham, he took over the role of senior professional but it was not the happiest of ways to gain recognition after his seven years in the team.

As for the Test, Cowdrey again won the toss to make it a clean sweep in the series and England proceeded to use up nearly two full days in totalling 393 all out. Pullar was dismissed soon after play began but Cowdrey and Dexter moulded the innings into shape with a stand of 191 and with another century to his credit Cowdrey was the domineering force. At the end of the first day a strange incident took place which spotlighted again the rather dubious decisions umpires at times made in the Caribbean. It began when Barrington was struck a painful blow on the arm off the fifth ball of the last over of the day from Hall.

Barrington decided he could not continue and when he left the field, retired hurt to all intents and purposes, all the other players did likewise, it obviously being decided that there was not sufficient time for a new batsman to take the crease. On the following morning Barrington declared himself fit enough to bat but at this the umpires intervened and would have none of it. They ruled that a new batsman must replace Barrington and he could not continue until a wicket had fallen. That is an interpretation of the law in its strictest sense but as no new batsman had actually replaced Barrington in the first instance it appears that the point was stretched a little too far when the law was applied so vigorously.

When the England innings ended Trueman began his attack on the West Indian batsmen in explosive style. Two separate incidents occurred, both involving Trueman, which set the home side's hopes well back. First, he hit Hunte with a bouncer causing a wound that required stitching and the batsman's immediate retirement from the innings. Then, when bowling to Alexander, he was very fortunate to run out McMorris, West Indies' second opening batsman. Trueman bowled and Alexander drove the ball back very straight and extremely hard. The ball struck Trueman's foot, ricocheted on to the stumps and the helpless McMorris was run out as he backed up for a single. That was the only wicket to fall and in the time remaining West Indies moved on to 49 for 1 to leave the sides evenly balanced after two days' play.

At this point a result appeared perfectly feasible to either side but by the end of the third day this hope had receded significantly. The weather played some part in this, a period of two hours being lost to rain, while West Indies batsmen also had a hand in affairs. In the three hours play that were possible they scored only 101 runs to finish at 150 for 2, barely halfway to England's total, and a draw became the ever-increasing likeliest possibility. On the fourth day the total advanced to 215 for 3 before Trueman and Moss brought about a mini-collapse, taking three wickets for 15 runs, and at this sudden transformation Hunte re-emerged to continue his innings. He raised his personal score to 72 not out but West Indies failed to gain a first innings lead and when Alexander declared at 338 for 8 they were still some 55 runs adrift. For Trueman the tour was proving to be a strenuous passage. Again he had a century of runs taken off his bowling but, at the figures reveal, he was having to work hard for his side and it was not surprising a high number of runs were scored off him at times when considering the number of overs he was sending down. His figures for the first innings read: 37.3–6–103–2.

Following his first innings century it was Cowdrey's turn to be dismissed cheaply when England batted again. Opening bowler Hall strained his back bowling the first ball but despite this incapacity he lulled Cowdrey into giving a gentle catch off the third delivery. The injury was severe to Hall and it also had a profound effect on his team. He was able to bowl only four overs from three separate spells in the entire innings, thus depriving West Indies of the most valuable attacking asset in the field and England's task of holding on for the draw was greatly simplified. Until the afternoon session of the fifth day this objective appeared to be a reasonably safe wager. Pullar, with nightwatchman Allen, added 65 runs to the score but after lunch three wickets fell cheaply. Had it not been for some rare poor fielding by West Indies, England's plight would have been far worse. Yet, despite the fielding lapses England were still only 203 ahead when Parks joined Smith at 148 for 6 and, ominously, the pitch was becoming more and more receptive to spin.

To England's delight, the situation improved radically after tea instead of worsening as was thought to be the most likely outcome. The new ball was due at that stage of the innings and after a short interlude for rain Alexander decided to take it. In the forty-five minutes remaining until the close of play the batsmen hammered 60 runs and in doing so changed the whole complexion of the game. This was a preview of a similar position England were to be in some four years later against Australia when Titmus was taken off for Trueman. The events then, described in Chapter Fourteen, were of a far more serious consequence both for Trueman personally and for England but generally the outcome was the same and a possible victory chance was lost, though in the case of West Indies the actual Test was not lost.

On the final day Parks and Smith continued on their merry way and took the record-breaking partnership on to 197 runs with Parks scoring his maiden Test century. Cowdrey delayed his declaration until after lunch, setting West Indies the impossible target of scoring 140 runs an hour to win and England were in an impregnable position to gain their first-ever win in a rubber in the Caribbean. With the pitch taking so much spin there was a slight possibility of England attempting to bowl out West Indies in their second innings but victory was only of secondary importance. With a one-nil lead in the series Cowdrey's task was to ensure against defeat and this he did, irrespective of how pointless his declaration was to the watching world.

Port of Spain brought the series to an end, a series that began amid much trepidation and forecasts of gloom. The players had brought back the perfect answer, albeit by the narrowest of margins, and none could be more pleased than Trueman. His part in the tour had been by no means a minor role. Throughout the series Trueman had been an integral component of England's team and his success in the first innings of the Second Test had been instrumental in bringing about the eventual victory. To a great extent the bowling had depended upon Trueman and Statham because on the hard, true pitches of the Caribbean Moss, the main support bowler, was never fast enough to be effective. To make up for this, Trueman was at his best and also added a new weapon to his considerable armoury which he displayed at regular intervals throughout the tour. This extra string to his bow was his ability, seemingly at will, to produce a very fast swinging yorker. It was an uncanny habit, not seen a great many times prior to the tour, but it was one which caused the batsmen a great deal of trouble. Also, his reputation as a 'character' was beginning to grow and Trueman proved to be very popular with the crowds wherever he played. From some of his antics it would be seen that he was equally adept at entertaining as he was with his bowling.

The whole series was undoubtedly a great success for Trueman. His total of twenty-one wickets was a record for a West Indies–England rubber in the Caribbean and he was now just one wicket short of the next important milestone in his career, his 150th Test wicket. After a short spell of recuperation, following the tour, South African batsmen would be in Trueman's sights for the 1960 series in England and he could look forward to reaching the 150 mark in the First Test. Barring five days of rain, there appeared little else to stop Trueman achieving it and so continue his inexorable march towards the double century.

AVERAGES FOR 1959–60 SERIES *v* WEST INDIES: Five Tests, Played Five

Overs	*Mdns*	*Runs*	*Wkts*	*Ave*
220.3	62	21	549	26.14

Inns	*NO*	*Runs*	*HS*	*Ave*
8	2	86	37	14.33

Catches=6

Match results=West Indies 0, England 1, 4 Matches drawn.

Statistics
1 Total Test wickets=149
2 Total catches=38
3 Total runs=487
4 Total appearances=36

N.B. Highest Wicket-taker in series for fourth time in his career.

9 South Africa, at home, 1960

When analysing the pattern of results following the 1959–60 tour to West Indies it immediately becomes apparent that the England Test team was enjoying a particularly fine run of success. Had it not been for the terrible thrashing meted out by Australia on the 1958–9 tour the claim could have been made, with considerable justification, that England were cricket's unofficial world champions at that period of time. Defeat had been a conspicuously absent ingredient since the conclusion of the Australian tour and by the end of the West Indies rubber twelve consecutive Tests had been played by England without one adverse result.

This excellent sequence was not altogether unforeseen. Throughout the 1950s the potential had always been present but it was a case of several players flattering only to deceive and it was not until the latter stages of the decade that the fruit of the team was borne in the most productive fashion. The facts were that England had not lost a home series since 1950 (when West Indies triumphed three-one in a four-Test rubber) but counteracting this worthy sequence was the disconcerting number of individual games that were lost in the same period, especially abroad. This total was sufficiently high as to detract from the overall success obtained. However, with the dawning of the 1960 home season, defeat had become obsolete to the England team and by the end of the series with South Africa the unbeaten run had been extended to seventeen games.

While the opposition had not always been of the highest calibre in this time, with the exception of West Indies, there could be little argument against a record which showed ten wins and seven draws out of every Test played by England since February 1959. It was a fair reflection of a very successful side and while the 1960 series against the South Africans resulted in a comfortable three-nil win for England, with two games drawn, it was unfortunate that matters other than cricket, pure and simple, cast a dark cloud over the proceedings almost from the moment 'Jackie' McGlew's side arrived in England.

The whole tour was a controversial affair from start to finish and the sometimes stormy events took the polish off England's steady march towards a record number of consecutive Tests without defeat. There were several varying factors that brought about this rather curious tour but it would be true to say that, to a certain degree, the South Africans were responsible for causing by their own hand several of the problems which arose during their stay in the British Isles. First, came the apartheid policy favoured by the South African government and though it had nothing whatsoever to do with eleven people playing cricket the cricketers were made the target for strong vocal attack from opponents of the policy. Demonstrations were staged at numerous grounds where the tourists played and it cannot have produced the ideal environment for the side to give of its best on the field of play. Secondly, came the highly doubtful bowling action of their young paceman Geoff Griffin. Not for the first time had the South Africans embarked on a tour with a bowler possessing a suspect action but on this occasion it would not pass without official comment.

The direct consequence of this was that history was made in the Second Test of the series at Lord's when Griffin became the first bowler to be no-balled for throwing in a Test Match in England. Indeed, it was so rare an event that only twice before in eighty-three years of Test cricket had instances been recorded of umpires taking such action. One occasion had been relatively recent when England's Tony Lock was called during the First Test against West Indies on the 1953–4 tour but for the other instance one had to delve back to the dim and distant past of the nineteenth century. The year then was 1898 when Australian E. Jones was no-balled for throwing at Melbourne in a Test against England. With this antiquity in mind it was quite natural that when Griffin was called great controversy arose and the incident evoked much comment and criticism which was not always helpful to a delicate issue.

Another disappointing facet of the summer for the South Africans was that in the final reckoning the tour was a financial failure. Falling attendances were a noticeable feature and these were not entirely due to the anti-apartheid demonstrators. A more likely reason was the lack of an effective challenge by the South Africans and when the time came for them to return home they had barely covered their expenses. This, for a foreign side visiting England, was an extraordinary occurrence but one which aptly sums up the attitude of the public towards the 1960 South Africans.

Anti-apartheid, politics, a poor touring team, they were all reasons for a disappointing summer but without question the topic mainly to come under discussion was Griffin and his bowling action. Various suggestions were made in an attempt to find a solution to the problem, some obvious some not, but none proved effective. In theory, the simplest answer appeared to be that a replacement bowler should be sent for as soon as possible from South Africa. The South African management vetoed this idea after a discussion and instead Griffin went to A. R. Gover, the former Surrey and England fast bowler, for specialist coaching. Success continued to elude the unfortunate young man because even after this the first-class umpires were still not satisfied with the legality of his action and the sensational events of the Second Test brought matters to a head.

After being called for throwing it was a racing certainty that Griffin would have returned home immediately after the Second Test but in that very same match he performed an even more remarkable feat which had a profound effect on the South African announcement made following the match. Griffin achieved the rare distinction of claiming a Test Match hat-trick, being the first South African to perform the act in a Test and the first man from any country to do so at Lord's in a Test and this clearly swayed the decision taken by the South African camp as to what was to become of Griffin. They decided that while Griffin would not bowl on any future occasion during the tour he would remain a member of the touring party and it appeared an honourable solution to a vexing problem.

The South Africans had many adverse factors besieging them while attempting to get on and play cricket and if they were not enough they also had the twin menace of Trueman and Statham to contend with. The pair complemented each other perfectly throughout the series and they dominated the South African batting to such an extent that they claimed nearly two-thirds of the wickets to fall in the five Tests. Their combined total for the series was fifty-two wickets out of the seventy-nine that fell to the bowlers, showing clearly their superiority not only over the batsmen but over the other English bowlers as well. Moss managed nine wickets in two games, Dexter five in five while the remaining thirteen went to the spin bowlers over the course of all five Tests. It was definitely a year for the fast bowlers. Normally, Trueman's total of twenty-five would easily qualify him for first place in the list of wicket-takers but Statham denied him this honour by claiming twenty-seven victims and in reality Trueman actually came third in the list. This was because the South African opening bowler Neil Adcock took twenty-six wickets. Under the trying conditions the nature and course of the tour presented to the visitors this performance was nothing short of brilliant by the South African and in some ways could be classed as more noteworthy than either Statham's or Trueman's own meritorious efforts. They did have each other to work with whereas Adcock, once Griffin became unavailable, was fighting a virtual lone battle and he stuck to his task with admirable grit and determination.

The venue for the series to begin was Edgbaston, a ground where England had yet to lose a Test. For Trueman the match marked an important stepping-stone on his march into the history books if he could secure a single wicket in either South African innings. With such solitary success his total of Test Match wickets would clear the 150 mark and the real records would begin to loom into sight. He would take a good deal more than one wicket in the match but when England batted first the arrival of his first wicket of the game was postponed until the second day's play. The short delay mattered little. As surely as night follows day the much vaunted wicket came with the following scorebook entry:

D. J. McGlew c Parks b Trueman 11

That wicket meant Trueman was nearly halfway to his final total of Test Match wickets. It had taken him eight years to achieve, almost to the day, 5 June 1952–10 June 1960 and had come in a total of thirty-seven appearances for England. In terms of averages his wickets had come at the rate of four per game but there had been slight fluctuations to this trend over the course of his career to date.

The first 50 wickets had arrived in 10 Tests while the second 50 took up 15 Tests. This makes the average recede from 5 in the first instance to approximately 3.3 in the second instance but everything works out very evenly at 4 wickets per game when noting that the first 100 wickets came in 25 Tests. With the third 50 wickets requiring 12 Tests this average of 4 was adequately maintained but there is rather more to it than would appear at first sight. In fact, there was a rise in the number of wickets per game when comparing the third 50 with the second 50 and gradually this proportion would continue to rise. As time progresses an amazing feature of Trueman's career will be seen to emerge that is a direct result of this observation; namely, that he was taking Test wickets at a far greater rate in the latter stages of his career than at any other time previously. There is a point to be remembered at this stage, however, in that Trueman's final total of 307 wickets should ideally be counted in blocks of 100, not blocks of 50. In that way the 50th, 150th and 250th wickets became milestones and nothing else. As a preliminary guide to averages the first three groups of 50 wickets give an interesting side light to Trueman's accumulation of Test Match victims but to use such groups throughout his career will give a very confused picture and one which will vary wildly from time to time. By using groups of 100 wickets at a time a much more regular pattern will emerge and it will also give a far truer indication as to the actual ratio of wickets to games that Trueman reached in the various stages of his career.

Once the wicket of McGlew was safely acquired in the First Test Trueman did not rest on his laurels. In a reasonably easy 100 run victory Trueman enjoyed a fine all-round match with some steady, purposeful bowling in both innings and a spirited innings when England batted a second time. His bowling figures were practically identical for each South African innings, being 24.5–4–58–4 and 22–4–58–3 respectively, while his quick-fire 25 with the bat was equally well worth watching in England's second innings. It included 16 in one over off Tayfield and although it was not his highest Test score the knock certainly showed up well when compared with the effort of Smith in the same innings. Trueman's sortie at the bowling lasted just twenty-two minutes while Smith laboured to 28 in two-and-a-half hours!

The series was away to a flying start for Trueman, but Lord's and the Second Test brought a swift reduction in the tempo from his point of view. Conversely, Statham stepped up to deliver a superb piece of bowling spread throughout the game to claim match figures of 11 for 97 and so became the first English fast bowler to take more than ten wickets in a Test since the war. In the first innings he had figures of 6 for 63 while Trueman failed to take a single wicket off thirteen overs and the second innings bore much the same markings. Statham's 5 for 34 once more outshone Trueman's 2 for 44 and it was the familiar pattern repeating itself of one or the other, never both at the same time, always taking the majority of the wickets to fall to the fast bowlers. It was brilliant, sustained pace bowling by Statham, giving a great deal of impetus to England's handsome victory by an innings and 32 runs but events bordering on the sensational occurred during the match which tended to cover over Statham's exploits.

Trueman had hardly managed to trouble the scorers in the Second Test and Statham performed magnificently but it was South African Griffin who captured all the headlines. Several incidents centred around the 21-year-old South African but the most startling came in England's only innings when he was no-balled eleven times by umpire F. Lee, standing at square-leg, and each occasion was for throwing. Quite naturally this caused great consternation in the South African camp. Also, in addition to being the first bowler ever to be called for such an offence in a Test in England, Griffin suffered further humiliation in an exhibition game which was hastily arranged when the Test Match proper finished unusually early.

The second umpire, J. S. Buller, had not had the opportunity to scrutinise Griffin's action from square-leg during the Test. He did in the exhibition match and the outcome of his vigilance was that he called Griffin four times for the same offence: throwing. The situation came to a farcical conclusion when Griffin completed his over bowling underarm. South African skipper, McGlew, had spoken to Buller and suggested this course of action, probably in the earnest hope to have the matter finished with once and for all and remove Griffin from the firing-line as soon as possible, yet even this did not satisfy the ever-alert umpires. Lee promptly no-balled Griffin again for failing to notify the batsman of his change of action and so reduced the state of play to the level of comic opera. Rules are rules, but this was only an exhibition game and by actions such as these umpires imply that they attach too much self-importance to their judicial powers when overseeing matches that are, in essence, nothing more than a knockabout.

Whatever trials and tribulations Griffin suffered in the game he was destined to make one more piece of history that he could always look upon with pride. Despite coming under the eagle eye of umpire Lee, Griffin performed the rare feat of taking a hat-trick in a Test Match. After all his toil and trouble it was poetic justice of a kind that his name should go into the record books for another, much happier, reason other than throwing.

Trueman never achieved the Test hat-trick in his career; therefore it is somewhat ironical that of the two he was privileged to witness in his fourteen years at the top he was an integral part of both. The first we have already seen described in Chapter Five when he caught the second of Peter Loader's three victims against West Indies in 1957. Now, three years later, Trueman was to be the vital third link in Griffin's notable triumvirate. The three wickets came as follows:

ENGLAND 1ST INNINGS

M. J. K. Smith	c Waite	b Griffin	99
P. M. Walker		b Griffin	52
F. S. Trueman		b Griffin	0

As with everything else concerning this Test the hat-trick was not a straightforward affair. Mike Smith went first, caught behind off the last ball of an over and Goddard bowled the next over to Walker. The Glamorgan batsman crashed two sixes over long-leg to reach his half century but when he got to the other end ready to face another Griffin over his innings was succinctly concluded. This brought Trueman striding to the wicket in his usual jaunty manner. He was not distracted at all by the South African's objective. Judging by his stroke at the delivery he received he believed he had the ideal solution required to deal with Griffin and had Trueman's flailing bat connected with the ball it would doubtless have sailed many a yard. Unfortunately, that did not happen. Trueman's middle stump was sent reeling and Griffin, just three weeks over twenty-one, had an undisputed claim to fame (rather than infamy) to take home with him at the end of a sad tour.

Amid the continuing debate on the unusual events of the tour the series moved on to Trent Bridge for the Third Test. Trueman bounced back to his form of the First Test and had another excellent match but all three English fast bowlers emerged with creditable figures. Between them Trueman, Statham and Moss claimed eighteen of the twenty wickets to fall (this was every wicket to fall to the fast bowlers as the remaining two batsmen were both run out) and while Trueman's star shone the brightest with nine wickets overall the overriding superiority of all the pace bowlers were clearly evident. Statham finished the match with five wickets, Moss with four and it marked one of England's best combined efforts by the front line bowlers in many years.

For the third consecutive time in the series Cowdrey won the toss. The usual decision to bat was taken and the first innings, totalling 287, lasted seven hours. That length of time provided a stark contrast when the South Africans made their first effort at the crease and in ten minutes under three hours they were dismissed for a dismal 88, their lowest score in England for thirty-six years. The total was the lowest ever recorded for a complete Test innings at Nottingham though mercifully for the South Africans was a little higher than the 30 they had mustered at Edgbaston in 1924.

The England attack was comprised entirely of pacemen. Trueman and Statham did the bulk of the bowling with Moss providing able back-up support and the South Africans were helpless in the face of such an onslaught. A mere 38.3 overs were required by the three bowlers to see the innings through from start to finish and this scintillating piece of work must rank as one of the best combined efforts by an England pace attack in the whole of Trueman's Test career.

Trueman and Statham in particular were in devastating form and the rout of the innings began in the very first over. McGlew was caught behind, fending away a rising ball from Trueman off the last delivery of his opening over. From that calamitous start the South Africans were never able to effect a recovery. O'Linn went next, brilliantly caught by Walker again off Trueman and then Statham joined the act to dismiss McLean and Wesley with successive deliveries. With the latter's departure half the side was out for 33, a disastrous position for any team to be in and the collapse continued unabated. Statham had come on to bowl at Trueman's end but this did not deter the rugged Yorkshireman. He roared back to snap up the last three wickets, all clean bowled, to complete a brilliant spell of bowling that was all-out attack from the first delivery yielding a fine analysis of 5 for 27. Indeed, it is well worth noting the analyses of all three bowlers. The manner in which they performed, in perfect harmony, is worthy of the record.

ENGLAND *v* SOUTH AFRICA: THIRD TEST MATCH AT TRENT BRIDGE 7, 8, 9, 11, 12 July 1960

SOUTH AFRICA: 1ST INNINGS

D. J. McGlew	c Parks	b Trueman	0
T. L. Goddard	run out		16
S. O'Linn	c Walker	b Trueman	1
R. A. McLean		b Statham	11
P. R. Carlstein	c Walker	b Statham	2
C. Wesley	c Subba Row	b Statham	0
J. P. Fellows-Smith	not out		31
J. H. B. Waite	c Trueman	b Moss	1
H. J. Tayfield		b Trueman	11
J. E. Pothecary		b Trueman	7
N. A. T. Adcock		b Trueman	0
	Extras	b 4 lb 4	8
			88

FALL OF WICKETS

1	*2*	*3*	*4*	*5*	*6*	*7*	*8*	*9*
0	12	13	33	33	44	49	68	82

BOWLING	*O*	*M*	*R*	*W*
Trueman	14.3	6	27	5
Statham	14	5	27	3
Moss	10	3	26	1

There was still about two hours' playing time left on the second day when South Africa followed on 199 runs behind and, although bad light followed by rain brought a premature close to the day after an hour, England had once more made steady inroads into the tourists' batting line-up. When play was halted the score stood at 34 for 3 and it appeared to be a foregone conclusion that the match would be speedily wound up on the third day. The South Africans decided otherwise. On the Saturday they all batted with a staunch tenacity which belied their previous form, especially McGlew, O'Linn and Waite, and in what was easily their best batting display of the series the South Africans not only took the game into the fourth day but made certain that England would have to bat again to secure victory.

McGlew showed his best form of the summer, looking the class batsman he was for the first time until, in very unfortunate circumstances, he was run-out. He was at the non-striker's end at the time and the incident took place when O'Linn played a ball from Moss towards Statham at extra-cover. The batsmen set off for a quick, yet reasonably safe single at which Moss dashed instantly across the pitch towards the ball. Meanwhile, McGlew was setting off for the single from the same end of the wicket and inadvertently ran into the back of Moss. McGlew stumbled, recovered, then dashed for the crease but by that time Statham had gathered the ball and shattered the stumps with unerring accuracy. The English players promptly appealed at this with the obvious outcome of umpire Elliott, at square-leg, having no hesitation in raising his finger and thus signifying McGlew's dismissal.

Moss had definitely not baulked McGlew deliberately; therefore the run-out decision was quite correct, but the crowd immediately made known their opinion of the incident in most vociferous terms as McGlew made his way back to the pavilion. This protest finally registered with Cowdrey for he called out for his opposite number to return to the crease. In fact, he called out three times but it was all to no avail for when the South African skipper did not go back the umpires would not hear of reversing the decision. The law was quite clear and once a decision had been given it was impossible to alter it; therefore McGlew had to go.

The umpires could not be faulted for taking this stand but in reality they should not have been placed in the predicament from the outset. It is all well and good to hold the view that a Test Match is far too serious a business to allow such gentlemanly ethics as sportsmanship to be practised in a manner which would have allowed McGlew time to complete the single but there are methods of obtaining wickets other than by means of default, no matter how unintentional the accident may have been. The reason for this is quite simple. Four years later the very same type of incident was to occur, under exactly similar circumstances, but with two vital differences. The roles would be reversed in so far as England would be batting at the time and also the opposition would not be South Africa but those deadliest of rivals—Australia. Moreover, the graceful, benevolent outcome of the 1964 affair would be an object lesson in sportsmanship which England needed to view with a special intent as the description to follow in Chapter Fourteen will perfectly illustrate.

With McGlew's dismissal in the Third Test South Africa's hopes of saving the game received a severe set-back, but his partner, O'Linn, did not appear to be too distressed by the incident. He continued a fine innings undeterred and found another valuable partner in Waite who scored a brave 60, but once he was out South Africa's last remaining chance of continuing the fight had gone. O'Linn was the last man to be dismissed, just two short of a maiden Test century, but it was sufficient, with the aid of Waite's contribution, to ensure that England would have to bat a second time.

Trueman had to work considerably harder for his reward in the second innings. He pounded down twenty-two overs to take

4 for 77 and coupled with his earlier success it added up to a fine match with nine wickets to his credit. The runs required by England amounted to no more than 49. An eight-wicket victory was a formality and it made the third consecutive season that England had clinched a home series in three straight games: 1958, New Zealand; 1959, India; and now 1960, South Africa and the unbeaten run was taking on a very, very impressive hue.

When England avoided defeat at Old Trafford in the Fourth Test the team established the longest unbeaten sequence in their history. Heavy rain washed out play on the whole of the first two days and a draw became a formality with only three days' play left. Cowdrey won the toss again and England totalled 260 all out but this was almost matched by the South Africans who made 229 all out, the innings being concluded late on the fourth day. Trueman had some early success in the innings, in harness with Statham, to have the South Africans struggling at 92 for 5. Another wicket then could have given England a grip on the game but a splendid century from McLean stifled the home side's chances. From twenty overs Trueman picked up 3 for 58 and they were his only wickets of the match.

In England's second innings, Cowdrey delayed his declaration until much too late, setting the South Africans 185 in less than two hours. It gave neither side any chance of forcing a victory and the South Africans were content to play out time, reaching 46 without loss. Trueman had a quiet game, apart from a few typical heavy-handed strokes when batting (he made 10 and 14 not out in the two innings) and it appeared as if the season's work was beginning to tell on him as the summer drew to a close. This was confirmed when he was rested from the Yorkshire side which played the tourists a week before the Fifth Test but when the final Test did get under way both Trueman and Statham appeared to be rather lethargic and it was obvious they needed a period of recuperation to recharge themselves at the end of a hard season.

In many ways the final Test, at the Oval, was the best match of the series. Events began with Cowdrey setting a unique record when he won the toss for the fifth consecutive time against McGlew and, in all, it made ten consecutive Tests in which England had gained choice of innings: five against South Africa and five the previous winter against West Indies. Cowdrey took the accepted decision to bat but on this occasion England derived no benefit from this course of action. There was intermittent rain throughout the first day's play which caused six separate stoppages and as a result the pitch was always in a lively state. Geoff Pullar, who had an outstanding match, was the only batsman to achieve a reasonable score, making 59 out of a moderate total of 155 all out by England and South Africa held an early advantage.

The South Africans did not fail to capitalise on the success of their bowlers when they began clearing the deficit. Caution was more in evidence than attack but while the tourists batted slowly (the innings lasted ten-and-a-quarter hours) they made certain of avoiding defeat by amassing 419 all out. A curious feature of this large total was the absence of a century from any of the South African batsmen. Goddard was the nearest to achieving the coveted three-figure score but he fell to a slip catch off Statham when just one run short of a maiden Test century.

Neither Trueman nor Statham were particularly effective in the South African innings. It was impossible for them to perform in a world-class manner in every game they played and their figures of 2 for 93, Trueman, and 1 for 96, Statham, show aptly how the signs of tiredness were creeping into their game. The one consolation for Statham was that his single victim, Goddard, took him past Jim Laker's total of 193 Test wickets. Only two bowlers remained ahead of him while Trueman was still some way behind, with twenty-one wickets less than Statham.

The tourists had a first innings lead of 264 runs but on the fourth day England wiped out this advantage with some cricket of a vintage rarely seen in a Test Match. The effort came from two batsmen, openers Pullar and Cowdrey, who put together a wonderful first-wicket partnership of 290. It was the highest such partnership for any Test ever played in England and its worth is easily discernible when it is also noted that on only four previous occasions in the history of the game had higher first-wicket stands been accumulated in Test Matches. These were 413 by Mankad and Roy at Madras in 1955–6 when playing for India against New Zealand, 382 by Simpson and Lawry in Barbados in 1965, when playing for Australia, 359 by Hutton and Washbrook at Johannesburg in 1948–9, and 323 by Hobbs and Rhodes at Melbourne in 1911–12. The individual scores for Pullar and Cowdrey were 175 and 155 respectively but following their supreme example the rest of the English batting was unimaginative.

The final total in England's second innings was 479 for 9 declared but the target set by Cowdrey, 216 in three hours, was never one that the South Africans would make a serious attempt at reaching. After the openers, no other England batsman reached 50 and the only player to put bat to ball in a workmanlike manner was Trueman. His 24 included 16 in four deliveries from Pothecary but by this time the game was already well on the way to a draw. The weather had the final word, rain shortening play on the last day with the South African score standing at 97 for 4, and, as at Manchester, the South Africans had finished the game in a reasonable position. After the failures in the earlier Tests the results at Old Trafford and the Oval could be appraised in terms of success, despite both games being drawn, and the South Africans would not be sorry to be returning home at the end of a depressing and frustrating tour.

The series was a complete success for England. Emphatic victories were gained in each of the first three Tests with notable contributions coming from Statham and Trueman. World records were beginning to loom ahead for both bowlers now but in this particular chase Statham held a slight advantage. At the end of the series the Lancastrian's total of Test wickets was 196, some twenty-two ahead of his Yorkshire rival. The next objective for Trueman was the double-century barrier. Once that was reached it would give added impetus to his challenge on the most important goal—Alec Bedser's world record of 236 Test wickets. It was a distinct possibility for Trueman who stood fifth in the all-time list of wicket-takers at the end of 1960 but there was one slight hurdle in his path. Of the four listed above him, one was still playing regular Test cricket.

The list was comprised of the following names: Bedser, 236 wickets; Statham, 196 wickets; Laker 193 wickets; Barnes 189 wickets; Trueman 174 wickets. The record was there for the taking but Statham was full of health and vigour and he wanted the world record just as much as Trueman did. Moreover, with his sizeable lead over Trueman, Statham had to be favourite to win the race but, none the less, the race would still be an exciting one to watch.

The pair could look forward to a respite from the gruelling circuit of Test cricket in the winter of 1960–1. There was not an official MCC tour planned for that winter and after nearly three years of non-stop cricket, summer and winter, home and abroad, this was not a bad arrangement. The Australians were due to visit England in 1961 and it was of the utmost importance that England's leading bowlers were fully refreshed for the start of the following series.

Since 1958 the England players had been playing cricket non-stop right through to the end of the 1960 series against South Africa. Two strenuous tours were undertaken during this period and, in effect, five seasons of cricket had been crammed into three years' actual playing time. The series were: New Zealand, 1958; Australia and New Zealand 1958–9; India, 1959; West Indies, 1959–60; and South Africa 1960. These series covered twenty-seven official Tests played by England of which Trueman had played in twenty-five. He missed only the First and Second Tests in Australia and had been ever-present since then, making for twenty consecutive appearances, and there could be little doubt that Trueman needed a winter's rest to recharge his batteries.

AVERAGES FOR 1960 SERIES *v* SOUTH AFRICA: Five Tests, Played Five

Overs	*Mdns*	*Runs*	*Wkts*	*Ave*
180.3	31	508	25	20.32

Inns	*NO*	*Runs*	*HS*	*Ave*
8	1	99	25	14.14

Catches=4

Match results=England 3, South Africa 0, 2 Matches drawn.

Statistics
1 Total Test wickets=174
2 Total catches=42
3 Total runs=586
4 Total appearances=41

10 Australia, at home, 1961

The Australian tour to England in 1961 was one of virtual uninterrupted success for the visitors and brought about England's first defeat in a home Test series since 1950. From the outset captain Richie Benaud stated his policy would be one of attack, a promise which was more than fulfilled, setting the tone for many exciting matches and, more importantly, only one defeat for the Australians. They had arrived in England with the Ashes already in their possession following their resounding home triumph three years earlier. As always, they had no intention of giving up the prize without a fight and while they were not the most formidable side to embark from down under the team was still good value for the two-one victory gained in the series.

The controversial question of throwing continued to be a major talking point, but due to a number of circumstances, the problem was never allowed to get out of hand. It was well known that Australia had players with suspect actions but, unlike South Africa in 1960, these players were not included in the touring party. It was less than a year since the ill-fated South African tour of England with the unfortunate Griffin amongst their ranks but, in sharp contrast to 1960, an amazing 'truce' was agreed upon between the authorities concerned that lasted for the first five weeks of the season. With Australia leaving behind their suspect bowlers the question of throwing was never likely to arise in any case but the 'truce' precluded the possibility whether or not any throwers were in the touring party. This was because the arrangement agreed was that if any umpire thought a bowler was throwing he would not be no-balled but a report would be forwarded to Lord's as an alternative. With Australia having no worries at all on this score, none of their players fell foul of the agreement and now that a possible contentious issue was safely out of the way all appeared set fair for an enjoyable summer.

With the exception of some very cold winds during May the weather was generally good and this favoured the Australian batsmen, batting being their main strength throughout the tour. Lawry, O'Neill, Harvey, Simpson, Burge and Booth all scored prolifically which was just as well for Australia's cause because for much of the time they were without the services of Benaud. He was a key bowler in the side, in addition to being captain, but suffered a great deal from a shoulder injury. This prevented Benaud from bowling in his orthodox style and whenever he did bowl the action subjected him to a great deal of pain.

As a result an added responsibility was placed on the shoulders of vice-captain Neil Harvey. He took charge of the team for the Second Test, which the Australians won handsomely, and proved more than equal to the task, leading the side well whenever called upon to do so. Harvey's greatest asset to aid him in this task was experience. This was his fourth (and final) trip to England and it was a blessing for the tourists that Benaud had such a capable deputy at his disposal for a series that was always fiercely contested, perhaps with more determination than if either side had been playing any other Test team in the world.

Thursday 8 June was the appointed day for the teams to get down to the serious business of winning, losing or retaining the Ashes and the chosen venue was England's happy hunting ground, Edgbaston. Defeat had never occurred in a Test there for England though the last occasion on which Australia had been in opposition at the Warwickshire headquarters was more than fifty years previous, 1909 being the date. Peter May was still not available to return to the England side and the captaincy remained in the hands of Colin Cowdrey who continued his extraordinary good luck with the toss. Benaud called wrongly to give England the choice of batting or fielding yet again, the eleventh consecutive time this had happened. The pitch was rather green, giving some hope of early help for the bowlers but Cowdrey decided to risk batting first.

The poor weather did not make for entertaining cricket and the first interruption came after just fifteen minutes' play. This set the pattern for the rest of the day but an end result of 180 for

8 had to be classed as a disappointing performance by England. Wickets fell regularly in between the showers with Subba Row the sole batsman to distinguish himself by staying two hours fifty minutes in making 59. He finally fell to Mackay, the third victim of a deadly four-ball spell by the bowler that shattered England's middle order and with the score at 156 for 8 the situation was perilous for the home side. Characteristically, Trueman came part way to his side's rescue with a typical hard hit innings of 20. It helped to carry the final score to 195 all out when the innings closed early on the second day but it was a long way short of being a reasonable total and Australia made rapid headway towards a first innings lead.

The Australian innings lasted the greater part of two days, Benaud withholding his declaration until 5.30 pm on the evening of the third day during which time the visitors accumulated a huge lead of 321 runs. With slightly more than two full days' play remaining England's hopes of saving the game appeared very remote and it was all credit to the Australians that they had played so well, thoroughly deserving to be in an almost unassailable position. Cowdrey varied his bowling in an attempt to stem the flood of runs but it made little difference to the Australian batsmen. At the end of the second day the score had raced to 359 for 5, an already substantial lead, and on the third day this was increased to 516 for 9 declared. Harvey was the architect of the innings with a well-controlled century, his fifth against England, and in very trying conditions the batsmen played particularly well. The weather was cold, wet and miserable but the Australians were able to maintain their scoring momentum over the eight-and-a-half hours that the innings lasted and for the English bowlers it was a frustrating time spent in the field.

Statham had the assistance of the wind for much of the time he was bowling and claimed 3 for 147 off 43 overs. Trueman bowled mainly against the wind to take 2 for 136 off 36.5 overs and it transpired to be his most unproductive efforts of the series. His first wicket did not materialise until his thirty-second over when he held a return catch to dismiss Simpson for 76 and he claimed the last wicket to fall when accounting for Grout but the heavy price, 136 runs, was the most runs he ever had taken off his bowling in a Test innings throughout his career. England did encounter a temporary set-back on the third day when wicket-keeper Murray received a nasty gash over the left eye. Illingworth pitched a ball into the bowler's rough which rose sharply but not being a bowler Murray's unfortunate departure from the field did not weaken England's attack. Neither did it make any difference to the Australians and they carried on much as they pleased until Benaud called a merciful halt with his declaration.

With such a huge score to make to ensure that Australia had to bat again the final hour the England openers had to survive on the evening of the third day was vital to their hopes of saving the game. It was imperative Pullar and Subba Row kept their wickets intact until the close but fortunately for England there was time for only two overs before bad light followed by rain stopped play for the day. It was the inclement weather that was eventually responsible for saving England when play resumed after the weekend break. The first wicket flourished to make 93 before Pullar was out five minutes before lunch on the fourth day. It was an infinitely better start than in the first innings but twenty minutes after lunch the rain returned and no further play was possible that day. On the last day, by courtesy of Dexter, England were never in danger of losing but how different the situation might have been had not the weather intervened on the fourth day is impossible to tell. With a deficit of 215 still before the England batsmen and over a day and a half left the odds had to be stacked on Australia's side. However, conjecture counts but little and the facts of the matter were vastly different.

The sun shone on the last day which brought forth the initial speculation that the pitch might favour the bowlers but Dexter proved this to be nonsense. In one of his finest-ever innings for England 'Lord Ted' was at his elegant best, scoring a supreme 180 in a stay at the crease lasting five-and-three-quarter hours. Dexter gave a masterly display of strokeplay and during his marathon effort he shared in two large partnerships. The first, with Subba Row, who also scored a century, was worth 109 followed by a second, larger partnership with Barrington which realised 161 runs. Pulls, drives, cuts—they all came alike to

Dexter who hit thirty-one boundaries in his innings and such was the strength of his batting that he was not dismissed until eight minutes from time on the final day. It was a marvellous show of tempered aggression by the Sussex captain which saved the day for England and by it the undefeated record at Edgbaston also remained intact.

At Lord's, in the Second Test, Australia made no mistakes when assuming a commanding position and catastrophically for England they cantered to an easy five-wicket win. After the match there was a heated controversy concerning the alleged ridge at the Nursery end. There was a certain amount of truth in this for the pitch was always lively, making the ball fly about alarmingly at times and several batsmen were struck disconcerting blows from deliveries which could not be classed as bumpers but, luckily, nobody was seriously hurt. The point to note is that over the five days' play the pitch was the same for the both sides and in the last reckoning it was Australia who overcame the conditions better than England. They were the better side on the day and no excuses should be put down to the state of the pitch for a somewhat lack-lustre performance by England, especially in the batting department.

May made his long-awaited return to the side but Cowdrey retained the captaincy and promptly continued his amazing sequence with the toss. For Australia, Harvey captained his country for the first time in his career in the absence of the injured Benaud and it was a most rewarding experience for him. In similar circumstances to Edgbaston, England derived no great benefit from winning the toss. By lunch on the first day, three wickets were down for 87, and this poor form with the bat continued right up to the tea interval with wickets falling in rapid succession. Once more the situation was desperate when Trueman went to the crease with the score at 164 for 8 and it was left to him and Statham to give the scoreline some semblance of respectability. They added 39 valuable runs for the last wicket, scoring 25, Trueman, and 11 not out, Statham, to raise the England score to 206 before the former was bowled by Davidson.

There was one hour left for the Australians to bat on the first day and, fresh from their batting exploits, Trueman and

Statham continued in a successful vein. They claimed one wicket each before close of play but it was Statham's success which evoked most excitement. A. Davidson b Statham 4 was the 200th Test wicket for the Lancashire stalwart and he became only the second Englishman to achieve such a total.

On the second day Australia recovered from the shaky overnight position to take the initiative by virtue of an excellent innings from Lawry who hit 130. England had a chance to assume command when the tourists were in danger of a second collapse but the balance of power once held was surrendered. Australia wavered slightly at 88 for 4 but the recovery was so intense that the last two wickets added 98 runs to give the tourists an overall lead of 134 runs. Trueman had another long stint of bowling in an innings which stretched into the third day and for the second consecutive match he had over 100 runs taken off his bowling but this time, unlike Edgbaston, the reward was more substantial, his figures reading 34–3–118–4.

England began batting a second time shortly after 1.00 pm on the third day. The score raced to 31 for 0 in the twenty-five minutes up to lunch, with Pullar contributing 24 of the runs, but at that point the flourishing strokeplay began to flounder. Four wickets fell rapidly after the interval and it was not until May and Barrington came together that a recovery became a possibility. They added 47, taking the score on to 127, when May was brilliantly caught one-handed by Grout and this meant England had just five wickets remaining when the lead was taken. By the close of play the score had advanced to 178 for 6, a lead of 42, but the last four wickets fell very cheaply on the fourth morning, setting Australia the simple task of scoring 69 runs to win. Once again, inept batting by England had cost the team dearly. For Grout, the Australian wicket-keeper, the match was also a personal triumph in addition to being on the winning side. He held five catches in England's second innings, eight altogether in the match, and amongst them was his 100th Test dismissal, giving an added gloss to a particularly fine performance.

The cause appeared hopeless for England, a mere practice session for Australia, but Trueman and Statham were far from finished yet and with the pitch retaining its liveliness the pair made full use of the helpful conditions. McDonald and Harvey went at 15, quickly followed by Harvey and O'Neill at 19 and had Lock managed to hold an extremely difficult chance from Burge off Trueman's last ball before lunch the impossible may just have happened. Had the chance gone to hand Australia would have been 35 for 5 but with so few runs for the bowlers to play with it was always an impossible task. Burge stifled any remaining English hopes after lunch by scoring 37 not out and although Statham took one more wicket the result was never in doubt. Nevertheless by taking the five wickets (Statham 3 for 31, Trueman 2 for 40) the pair had given the Australians plenty of food for thought in their second innings scramble for victory.

The Australians went to Headingley for the Third Test full of confidence following the Lord's win which put them one up in the series. Without warning they were blasted back to reality by one man—Trueman. Two separate spells of bowling, one in each innings, were all he needed to complete what was probably his finest-ever performance for England. The rout of India in 1952 had been very impressive, notably his 8 for 31 in the Third Test, but the achievement against Australia was in the face of a much stronger opposition who were far superior to the Indians in ability, technique and all round playing strength. Trueman was also destined to take comparable numbers of wickets against West Indies in 1963 in two consecutive Tests but, again, the Australian match has to be rated better because Trueman's match analysis in 1961 was substantially better than in either of the subsequent games against the Caribbean tourists. Quite rightly, the game was billed as 'Trueman's Match' and rarely can one man have decimated an international batting line-up with such devastating ferocity as Trueman did at Headingley in July 1961.

The drama did not begin to unfold until after tea on the first day. Up to that point Australia had apparently been coasting along to reach 183 for 2 without a sign of any description to show what lay in store. Prior to play commencing, May had resumed his role as captain only to lose the toss and so conclude England's astonishing twelve-match successful run with the coin and Australia took immediate heart at the prospect of batting first. Statham was a notable absentee from the England side and the selectors went for experience in their choice of replacement, the forty-year-old Les Jackson receiving a surprise international call-up.

The visitors progressed quite well, if a little sedately, up to the lunch interval. In this time Jackson proved his worth, bowling for an hour non-stop, as he was also to do after the interval, and in this two-hour session of play England's solitary success was the wicket of Lawry, leg-before to Lock. At the first break the score had reached a reasonable 77 for 1 and further satisfactory batting followed in the second session. Again, Lock was the only successful bowler, dismissing McDonald, while Harvey's presence was taking on a more and more ominous appearance as the day went by. The tea interval came with Australia firmly in command: Harvey 66 not out, O'Neill 27 not out.

The new ball was due shortly after tea and with it came Trueman's spell of pure bowling magic. O'Neill was the first to go, superbly caught by Cowdrey in the slips, then Harvey, equally well caught by Lock down by his bootlaces. Trueman was in full battle-cry now. Everything was slotting perfectly into shape, the rampant Trueman the crowd loved to see was bowling off his longest run, at his fastest, and the bewildered Australians did not know what had hit them. Simpson was the next to go, beaten by speed and trapped leg-before. This brought Benaud to the wicket but the Australian captain need not have bothered donning his pads. Trueman tore up to the wicket, Benaud hung out his bat in an apology of a stroke, over went the stumps and the Test Match hat-trick was on yet again. The outcome of that particular event was inevitable no matter how well Trueman was bowling but he was still not finished. Grout was caught behind in his next over and Trueman's first remarkable spell was at an end. In just six overs Trueman had claimed five wickets for 16 runs to finish with the final analysis of 5 for 58.

There was some spirited resistance at the end of the innings from Davidson and McKenzie who added 29 for the last wicket before Allen bowled McKenzie to claim his only wicket of the innings. In a matter of ninety minutes England, or more appropriately Trueman, had polished the eight remaining Australian wickets for the addition of only 54 runs. Incredibly, worse misfortune was to befall Australia in their second innings and it was to bring out an even better performance from Trueman.

Before that could take place England had to bat. Caution was the applicable password for the batsmen when they arrived at the crease and the ploy served England's purpose admirably. The first wicket put on 54, followed by 86 from the second and by tea-time on the second day the score had reached 176 for 2 but England did not relinquish their grip on the game as the Australians had done when in an identical position on the previous evening. Pullar batted three hours twenty minutes for 53 and while it was a slow rate of scoring, it was made to be by the indifferent bounce of the pitch. The best batting came from Cowdrey who made 93 in four-and-a-quarter hours and also from Lock on the third morning. Against the general trend of the English innings, Lock hammered 30 runs in seventeen minutes, flaying Benaud's bowling to all parts of the ground. All of Lock's runs came off the luckless Australian captain and included seven boundaries. When the innings closed, England were 299 all out and holding an advantage of 62 runs.

It was a slender lead and the prospect of batting fourth on an unpredictable wicket gave cause for some concern among English followers. The fears were unfounded. Trueman was hovering in the background, ready to tear the Australian batting to shreds again, although he did not do so straightaway. Jackson was the first to make his mark, bowling McDonald with the fifth ball of his first over. Neither did the second wicket go to Trueman. That went to Allen, who had Lawry caught behind off his first delivery of the innings when the score was 49. This brought O'Neill in to join forces with Harvey and, as in the first innings, they settled down to begin making steady progress against the English bowling.

May varied his bowling astutely in an attempt to make another breakthrough but Harvey was the apparent master of the situation. He did have one lucky escape when he was 10; May dropped a relatively easy chance in the gully off Trueman, but apart from that one lapse the Australian batted with great determination and composure. With O'Neill still his partner, Harvey took his side into the lead and not until Australia were

98 for 2 did May have his moment of inspiration that prompted him to recall Trueman to the attack.

O'Neill was facing and he gained an immediate single. Two balls later Harvey was on his way back to the pavilion, having been caught in the covers and the fall of that wicket signified the beginning of Trueman's most superlative burst of bowling in Test cricket. There cannot be any other way to describe a spell of bowling that lasted for just twenty-four deliveries and from which he claimed five wickets without conceding a run. Trueman went on to bowl at 3.40 pm and by 4.15 pm, the tea interval, Australia had crashed from 98 for 2 to 109 for 8. Beginning with Harvey, Trueman carried on to dismiss O'Neill, Mackay, Benaud (for his second nought of the match) and Simpson. Australia had been obliterated by the best spell of fast bowling seen in England for at least nine years (since Trueman's own devastation of the Indians at Manchester) and probably for a good deal longer than that.

If there was any secret to Trueman's phenomenal success it came after Harvey's dismissal. From bowling off his long run at full pace, Trueman reverted to his shorter run and bowled to a tightly set leg field. It was good captaincy on the part of May with Trueman doing the rest in his own inimitable style. To not concede a single run while taking five wickets placed him in the unplayable class and in the half-hour leading up to the tea interval this was undeniably true. The Australian batsmen had no answer at all to his accuracy, control and subtle change of pace. After the tea interval Jackson claimed a second wicket, holding a return catch from Grout, and Trueman rounded off the innings by having Davidson brilliantly caught in the slips by Cowdrey. It was his sixth wicket of the innings, only the second time he had taken more than five wickets in an innings in his forty-four Test career to date and at the end of the innings there were some remarkable figures for the analyst to study.

In all, Trueman's bowling in the Australian second innings could be split into four distinct sections. This gives four separate sets of bowling figures, the first of which came as Australia moved to 98 for 2; these were: 8–1–25–0. It was then that Trueman was brought on for his rapid-fire burst of 5 for 0 in twenty-four deliveries and so complete the second set of figures. As he continued after tea to conclude the innings there is a third set showing his full wicket-taking burst from the moment May brought him back into the attack and they were: 7.5–4–5–6. Add those to the first set and the final fourth analysis is for the complete innings; namely 15.5–5–30–6. The full scorecard reads as follows:

ENGLAND *v* AUSTRALIA: THIRD TEST MATCH AT HEADINGLEY
6, 7, 8, 10, 11 July 1961

AUSTRALIA:	1ST INNINGS			2ND INNINGS		
W. M. Lawry	lbw	b Lock	28	c Murray	b Allen	28
C. C. McDonald	st Murray	b Lock	54		b Jackson	1
R. N. Harvey	c Lock	b Trueman	73	c Dexter	b Trueman	53
N. C. O'Neill	c Cowdrey	b Trueman	27	c Cowdrey	b Trueman	19
P. J. Burge	c Cowdrey	b Jackson	5	lbw	b Allen	0
K. D. Mackay	lbw	b Jackson	6	c Murray	b Trueman	0
R. B. Simpson	lbw	b Trueman	2		b Trueman	3
A. K. Davidson	not out		22	c Cowdrey	b Trueman	7
R. Benaud		b Trueman	0		b Trueman	0
A. W. T. Grout	c Murray	b Trueman	3	c and b	Jackson	7
G. D. McKenzie		b Allen	8	not out		0
	Extras	b 7 lb 2	9	Extras	lb 2	2
			237			120

FALL OF WICKETS

1	*2*	*3*	*4*	*5*	*6*	*7*	*8*	*9*
65	113	187	192	196	203	203	204	208

BOWLING	*O*	*M*	*R*	*W*	*O*	*M*	*R*	*W*
Trueman	22	5	58	5	15.5	5	30	6
Jackson	31	11	57	2	13	5	26	2
Allen	28	12	45	1	14	6	30	2
Lock	29	5	68	2	10	1	32	0

Trueman's match analysis of 11 for 88 was the best of his career, although it was unfortunate that the pitch was heavily criticised after the game due to the uncertain bounce and various heights that the ball came off the wicket. There was no doubt that the pitch favoured the bowlers, both fast and slow, but from both sides there was only one, Trueman, who capitalised to the fullest extent on the conditions available. If the pitch had been in an unusually bad state more than one bowler would have netted a substantial haul of wickets but that did not materialise and Trueman had the stage all to himself.

Due to Trueman's monumental effort, England required a modest 59 runs for victory in the hour-and-a-half remaining for play. Pullar and Subba Row began carefully until the latter fell to Davidson at 14. Cowdrey joined Pullar to take the total to within 14 of the required 59 when Benaud had Cowdrey caught behind. This brought May to the crease and it was appropriate that England's captain should be at the crease when Pullar made the winning hit off Benaud with the time approaching 6.20 pm. The match was over with two full days to spare and Australia had suffered its first, and only, defeat of the season by eight wickets. Under the circumstances, however, they could be excused for claiming they had not been beaten by the England team but by one member of it almost single-handed—Fred Trueman.

Within a matter of weeks of his greatest ever triumph for his country Trueman was ignominiously thrown out of the England team in a fashion which bore all the hallmarks of his expulsion from the side in the mid 1950s. Trueman's run of twenty-four consecutive appearances was brought to an inglorious end despite his sensational exploits in the Third Test. What did Trueman do then that was so drastic as to cause his instant removal from the side? In short, he was made a scapegoat, an occurrence not uncommon to Trueman at various stages of his career and on this occasion he was made to shoulder the blame for England's defeat in the Fourth Test at Old Trafford. Here was England's premier fast bowler, an ever-present in the national side for three full seasons (which was a run stretching back to January 1959 during which time he took 104 Test wickets), and because England were beaten Trueman was dropped.

The official cause of England's defeat was that Benaud, by bowling into rough patches made by the bowlers' follow-through, was able to cause a dramatic collapse when England batted a second time needing 256 runs to win the match. The person automatically credited with making the footmarks was Trueman but this should not be very surprising. He had been blamed for many things in the past and now, when England needed somebody to blame, it was logical that Trueman should be first in the firing line. It was hardly fair but many incidents appertaining to Trueman's conduct were dealt with in the same, succinct manner and as a result Trueman was dropped for the Fifth Test at the Oval. The two galling aspects of this decision is that it was made so soon after he had defeated the Australians virtually on his own at Headingley and also that no effort was made to ascertain the true facts because there are a number of reasons for believing that Trueman did not, in fact, create the much criticised footholds entirely by his own actions.

Trueman bowled a total of forty-six overs in the match and it is a definite fact that he did not bowl them all from the same end. This becomes apparent from the match account by *Wisden* which clearly corroborates the point: 'Simpson fell in Statham's first over and, switching ends, the Lancashire fast bowler also dismissed Harvey at 51'. Thus Trueman and Statham switched ends after bowling one over each from their respective opening berths. There were two more pace bowlers in the attack, in addition to Trueman and Statham, namely Flavell and Dexter, and at least one leading ex-England cricketer, who cannot be named, has every reason for believing that it was, in fact, Dexter who was the main culprit. However, the object of the exercise is not to apportion blame and while it is true to a certain degree that a bowler of Dexter's height, and with his action, would bring his front foot down from a greater height than any of the other bowlers the main point to observe is that there were four fast bowlers operating in the match, not just one, ie Trueman or Dexter to whom blame can be attached. Therefore, the safest appraisal is to put the cause of the footmarks down to a combination of the actions of all four pace bowlers and not state categorically that it was one or the other.

An interesting point to arise from the controversy is the veritable wall of silence encountered by the author when researching this particular episode in Trueman's career. With the exception of the previously mentioned ex-Test player, who must remain anonymous for obvious reasons (not least being professional integrity), nobody of any consequence was prepared to discuss the matter. The simplest solution to prove or disprove any theories would have been to view the recording made of the match by the BBC but this was turned down despite the author being prepared to bear the cost. A similar situation arose with MCC who apologetically decreed they could not help with the matter; the point being that while the scorebook might not have indicated which ends each bowler operated from it would not have needed a mathematical genius to deduce the facts had the figures been made available. The most reasonable suggestion towards a solution came from Mr W. Frindall, the eminent cricket historian and statistician, who proposed that the author contact the umpires concerned in the match. The one flaw to that course of action is the MCC ruling prohibiting all people under contract with the Board from discussing any particular aspect of the game with the media which may be used in publications and this made it pointless in making any contact with the officials concerned. All of which adds up to a rather bare picture of the actual events.

With the benefit of hindsight it is obvious that two vital events, at different stages of the game, are the clues as to why Australia won the match. First, was the last wicket partnership of 98 between Davidson and McKenzie in Australia's second innings and second was Benaud's inspired spell of bowling when he went round the wicket and aimed for the bowlers' footmarks in England's second innings.

Taking the match through its various stages from beginning to end it will be seen how these two events fall into place. Australia batted first but could total only a modest 190 all out which England had little difficulty in reaching. The first innings lead eventually stretched to 177, a lead of sufficient proportion to enable England to think in terms of an ultimate victory but the tourists were far from down and out and they hit back strongly in their second innings. A first wicket partnership of 113 helped them to clear the arrears for the loss of just two wickets and as the innings progressed each succeeding wicket made useful contributions to the score. This continued until the last morning when Allen made a vital breakthrough to claim three wickets in fifteen deliveries without conceding a run. This mini-collapse saw the Australian score slump from 331 for 6 to 334 for 9 and the tourists were on the verge of being all out.

At this point, Australia were only 157 runs ahead with the solitary wicket remaining and Davidson launched an immediate attack on Allen's bowling, taking 20 off one over. There began the last-wicket stand of 98 and from having the reasonably easy target of 160 or thereabouts to chase, England were confronted with the infinitely harder task of scoring 256 runs to win. More importantly, the last pair had not only added troublesome runs to the total but had also taken away valuable time from England's batsmen in the process. To win, England had to score the runs in 230 minutes, a rate of very nearly a run a minute, and that was a tall order for a Test Match, but by virtue of a brilliant innings by Dexter it could have been achieved.

Pullar and Subba Row gave the team a reasonable start before Dexter came to the crease to play an innings almost as good as his 180 at Edgbaston. It was a display of controlled hitting at its very best and put England in with a better than evens chance of winning. With the score standing at 150 for 1, Dexter had scored 76 in only eighty-four minutes and it was then that Benaud took his gamble. He began bowling round the wicket with immediate success and the wickets began falling like ninepins. For the addition of a meagre 51 runs the remaining nine English batsmen were hurried out to give Australia an emphatic victory which also meant they retained the Ashes. So rapid was Benaud's success that the position was hopeless for England by tea. Only Barrington remained of the recognised batsmen with a further 93 runs still required in eighty-five minutes. Consequently, when he was out it became a question of whether or not the tail-end batsman could hang on for a draw. The answer was negative. Davidson bowled Statham twenty minutes from the end and Australia had clinched the game.

As far as Trueman was concerned that was the end of the series for him. It was true that he had played a rather insignificant part in the match (one wicket for 147 runs out of both innings) but whether or not that was sufficient reason to drop, the footmarks business apart, is very much open to question. One swallow does not make a summer and one bad game does not mean the end of the road for England's leading bowler, especially when bearing in mind what he did when destroying the Australians at Headingley only weeks earlier. Yet the selectors, in their quest to apportion blame cast Trueman aside as if he counted but little towards the team. Ironically, Trueman could still have the last laugh. For the fifth time in his career he took more wickets in the series than any other English bowler and even the selectors could not dispute that fact!

AVERAGES FOR 1961 SERIES *v* AUSTRALIA: Five Tests, Played Four

Overs	*Mdns*	*Runs*	*Wkts*	*Ave*
164.4	21	529	20	26.45

Inns	*NO*	*Runs*	*HS*	*Ave*
6	0	60	25	10.00

Catches=2

Match results=England 1, Australia 2, 2 Matches drawn.
Statistics
1 Total Test wickets=194
2 Total catches=44
3 Total runs=646
4 Total appearances=45

N.B. Trueman was the highest English wicket-taker in a series for the fifth time in his career.

11 Pakistan, at home, 1962

Following the 1961 home series against Australia, MCC undertook a strenuous tour to India, Pakistan and Ceylon which lasted from early October 1961 until February 1962. Eight official Tests were played, five against India and three against Pakistan, but the format of the tour made for a curious, disjointed affair that involved a great deal of travelling. The original itinerary had to be drastically altered when India arranged a tour of West Indies beginning in February 1962 and this meant MCC had a strange timetable to follow in order to complete their own tour. Three first-class matches, including one Test, were played in Pakistan, when the tour began. Then followed the whole of the Indian part of the campaign with a five-Test series before returning to Pakistan to complete the programme. It was a far from ideal arrangement and although Trueman missed eight possible Test appearances by not participating on the tour (and almost certainly missed raising the double century of Test wickets as well) he was more than likely better off staying in England. A tour such as the one undertaken to the sub-continent in 1961–2 would sap the strength of the fittest of men and after a hard summer against the Australians combined with the prospect of going down under in the winter of 1962 it is probable that Trueman derived more benefit by missing the trip and resting up for the winter.

Hard on the heels of the excursion to the east, England was once more in direct opposition with Pakistan in the summer of 1962 with a full five-Test series on the programme. On this occasion the England players would meet the Pakistanis in a far more relaxed mood than the cramped course of the winter tour had allowed and, with the series being at home, the England selectors would have at their disposal all of the players who had missed the first venture. This obviously included Trueman, as well as players such as Cowdrey and Statham who had likewise not gone on the tour, and the 1962 series was to be the first and

Peter Burge is trapped l.b.w. by Trueman during Australia's first innings at Trent Bridge, 1964.

Ian Redpath, the Australian opener is bowled, also in the first innings. The batsman at the other end is Bill Lawry.

In the same innings O'Neill has a lucky escape as the ball evades Colin Cowdrey's outstretched arm.

only time Trueman would play Test cricket against Pakistan. They had toured England once before during Trueman's career, in 1954, but that was at a time when he had been out of favour with the selectors.

For the tour Pakistan were led by Javed Burki who had previously gained a fair measure of experience of English conditions while playing for Oxford University. He had achieved some notable successes with the Dark Blues but, on the whole, the 1962 series against England would not rank amongst the happiest moments of his short career. At the age of twenty-four Burki was somewhat younger than the majority of Test captains but that does not detract from his ability and despite the lack of any Test Match success in the series the Pakistanis were by no means a poor side. This estimation comes from Peter Parfitt who played in all five Tests and who had also taken part on the winter tour which embraced Pakistan in the programme. The results of Parfitt's play were favourable enough for him to become a regular member of the England team and having played against Pakistan both at home and abroad in such a short space of time gave Parfitt ample opportunity to assess their strengths and weaknesses.

The consequence of Parfitt's qualified opinion is that, by way of comparison, he rates them far superior to the Australian tourists to England in 1977 and equally as good as the same tourists of 1964 vintage. This would make the Pakistanis of 1962 a more than reasonable side, despite the fact that England strolled to a four-nil win in the series with the remaining game drawn and, on the face of it, the results would appear to be in complete contrast with Parfitt's train of thought. The most glaring contradiction is the suggestion that the tourists were equal to the 1964 Australians who came to England and won the series one-nil. However, it must be remembered that 1962 was something of a golden summer for Parfitt. He scored no less than five centuries against the Pakistanis and his judgement is based on first-hand experience gained by having played against both sides with more than a fair share of success. Therefore, it must be accepted that the Pakistanis were a far better side than the mere results of the Tests would indicate at first sight.

England's superiority over the tourists was evident from the beginning of the series which got under way at Edgbaston. Dexter won the toss and the England batsmen proceeded to accumulate their highest score, 544 for 5 declared, since 1957 when the West Indian bowlers had been hammered to the tune of 619 for 6 at Trent Bridge. A huge total was in prospect at the end of the first day. With the aid of a brilliant 159 by Cowdrey, made in four hours twenty-three minutes, England's total reached 386 for 4 and the Pakistani bowlers suffered in much the same vein on the second day. Graveney narrowly missed a century, being caught when 97, but the real highlight came from Parfitt and Allen who added a record 153 runs for the sixth wicket. Dexter declared at lunch, after Parfitt had reached his century and Pakistan began the daunting task of attempting to salvage the game.

The tourists were soon in trouble. Two wickets were down for 30 before two of the famous Mohammad brothers, Hanif and Mushtaq, staged a partial recovery with a partnership of 78 for the third wicket. It aided the cause a little but by the end of the second day Pakistan were struggling at 149 for 5, although early on the third day the situation began to improve again for the visitors. Dexter began with an all-spin attack, prolonging this tactic for an hour and it enabled the overnight batsmen, Imtiaz and Wallis, to raise the score past 200. It was not until the ninety-second over of the innings that Statham was recalled to the attack and with his first delivery he ended the sixth wicket partnership.

The breakthrough by Statham signified the end of the first innings for Pakistan. Trueman was also recalled and he promptly bowled Imtiaz with the score at 206, at which point two more wickets fell in rapid succession to the ever accurate Statham. There was a defiant flourish from the last pair which added 40 runs, including 24 in three overs from Trueman, but the position was hopeless for Pakistan. Shortly before lunch on the third day they were all out for 246 and a follow-on target of 298 runs did not augur well for the Pakistanis.

England were not extended to complete the match with more than a day to spare, the last wicket of the Pakistan second innings falling shortly after lunch on the fourth day, although the visitors did fare a little better when they batted again. The final victory margin was an innings and 24 runs giving England a good start to the series but for Trueman it was a quiet game and the double century of wickets did not materialise during the Test. He claimed four wickets altogether, 2 for 59 in the first innings and 2 for 70 out of a second innings total of 274 all out. The situation could only improve and at Lord's, in the Second Test, Trueman bounced back to his brilliant best.

There was a heavy, humid atmosphere on the first morning of the Lord's Test and with the pitch apparently favouring the seam bowlers, Burki took something of a gamble when he decided to bat first after winning the toss. Immediately, Trueman came to the fore. The conditions were ideal for him to demonstrate his talents to the full and bowling on a damp, green wicket he was lethal. Trueman ripped the heart out of the Pakistani batting. He bowled at top speed, was accuracy personified and swung the ball considerably and the Pakistani batsmen hardly knew which way to turn. The innings lasted just two-and-three-quarter hours, during which time Trueman claimed 6 for 31 off 17.4 overs. The analysis was the third best of Trueman's Test career to date but it was the second wicket of the sextet that he would prize the most. Overall, it was a brilliant, accurate piece of bowling but that second wicket was the much sought-after 200th victim.

Javed Burki c Dexter b Trueman 5

With the wicket Trueman became the sixth bowler to achieve the double century of wickets in Test cricket and he reached the milestone in less deliveries than any of the five who had gone before him. Counteracting this was the length of time Trueman had been forced to wait before finally reaching the goal. It was ten years exactly to the month since his international debut and but for his earlier banishment from the Test arena the 200 mark would surely have been reached much earlier than June 1962. On averages alone it would have materialised at about the time Trueman actually secured his 100th wicket at Christchurch in 1959 but plain facts carry more weight than hypothetical questions which can never be answered. However, other more tangible points do arise from Trueman's 200th wicket in Test cricket.

The double century was raised in Trueman's forty-seventh Test Match. This meant that the second 100 had been claimed in twenty-two Tests, three fewer than the first 100 had taken. Thus, the average number of wickets per Test was steadily improving, up from 4.0 to 4.7 per game but this is not surprising when considering that the second century came in the period 1959–62 which coincided exactly with Trueman's most consistent phase in the team, a run of twenty-four consecutive appearances for England. One point appears to balance the other out but this trend will be seen to continue for the third 100 arrived in even quicker time than either of the first two instances! The final century took only eighteen Tests, proving conclusively that Trueman was taking more Test wickets towards the end of his career than at any other time. Yet, the four years Trueman spent on the touchlines in the mid 1950s are generally thought to have been his prime years as a bowler. If they were, one can only marvel at the number of wickets he might have taken, given a fair chance in his earlier days.

The outcome of the rich haul Trueman took in the Pakistan first innings at Lord's was that Trueman's sights were firmly fixed on Alec Bedser's world record of 236 Test wickets. The six wickets had taken his total well past 200 and the full scorecard read as follows:

ENGLAND *v* PAKISTAN:
SECOND TEST AT LORD'S
21, 22, 23, 25, 26 JUNE 1962

PAKISTAN: 1ST INNINGS

Hanif Mohammad	c Cowdrey	b Trueman	13
Imtiaz Ahmed		b Coldwell	1
Saeed Ahmed		b Dexter	10
Javed Burki	c Dexter	b Trueman	5
Mushtaq Mohammad	c Cowdrey	b Trueman	7
Alim-Ud-Din		b Coldwell	9
Wallis Mathias		b Trueman	15
Nasim-Ul-Ghani	c Millman	b Trueman	17
Mahmood Hussain	c Cowdrey	b Coldwell	1
Antoa D'Souza	not out		6
Mohammad Farooq	c Stewart	b Trueman	13
	Extras	b 1 lb 2	3
			100

FALL OF WICKETS

1	*2*	*3*	*4*	*5*	*6*	*7*	*8*	*9*
2	23	25	31	36	51	77	78	78

BOWLING	*O*	*M*	*R*	*W*
Trueman	17.4	6	31	6
Coldwell	13	2	25	3
Dexter	12	3	41	1

Graveney dominated England's first innings reply. In an innings lasting four hours he scored 153 and was last man out with the England total on 370. Throughout his innings, Graveney received little support from the other batsmen with the exception of Trueman. The pair added 76 for the ninth wicket, a record for that wicket in England–Pakistan Tests, of which Trueman's share amounted to 29. The England lead stretched to 270 runs and when Pakistan lost four wickets for 77 in their second innings the match appeared to be heading for a speedy conclusion.

At the fall of the fourth wicket Burki was joined at the crease by Nasim-Ul-Ghani with half an hour remaining for play on the second day. They were not separated until well after lunch on the third day and they took their side into the lead in the process. Both batsmen scored centuries and their partnership, which realised 197 runs, was a record for Pakistan's fifth wicket in any Test and their highest by any wicket against England. Burki and Nasim batted fluently and their sterling performances ensured that England would have to bat a second time to gain the eventual victory. When the Pakistan innings closed at 355 all out, England required 86 to win with ninety minutes' play remaining on the third day.

The bowling honours in Pakistan's second innings went mainly to Coldwell, who took 6 for 85, compared to Trueman's 3 for 85 but their match figures were almost identical. Coldwell claimed 9 for 110, a notable performance on his Test debut, while Trueman ended the game with 9 for 116. Both fast bowlers had played extremely well, leaving few opportunities for the other bowlers and only Dexter and Allen, with one wicket apiece, managed to secure a wicket before Coldwell and

Trueman completed the rout. For the loss of Cowdrey, England scored the 86 runs required for victory in just sixty minutes to complete the match with more than two days to spare and by virtue of the nine-wicket win a decisive two-nil lead in the series was taken.

The Third Test, played at Headingley, followed much the same pattern as the previous game. Again, the match was completed with more than two full days remaining and the victory margin, an overwhelming innings and 117 overs, was England's most emphatic of the summer. At the beginning of the game such a resounding result did not appear at all likely but a combination of bad luck, dropped catches and injuries hampered the Pakistanis so badly that the team disintegrated.

Burki began by taking the unusual step of asking England to bat first after he won the toss. It was a wise move. There was a heavy atmosphere and a green pitch which greatly assisted the seam bowlers and Pakistan made rapid inroads into the England batting line-up during the first day's play which was cut short by an hour-and-a-half due to the inclement weather. The score at the close of play was 194 for 6, which reflected Pakistan's best day's play of the tour to date.

On the second day nothing went right for Pakistan. With Parfitt as the mainstay, the last four wickets added 248 runs to England's score with all the tail-end batsmen making valuable contributions. Murray, 29, Allen, 62, Trueman, 20, and Statham, 26 not out, all batted competently but it was Parfitt who dominated the issue. He hit eighteen fours in a fluent, well-paced innings which yielded him 119 runs. It was Parfitt's third century in four Tests against Pakistan and as if that were not enough he had yet to reach the peak of his form for that summer, especially against the tourists' long-suffering bowlers.

England's final score of 428 all out was a formidable proposition for the tourists who were seriously handicapped by an injury to Hanif Mohammad. He had a severely bruised knuckle and his place as opening batsman went to Alim-Ud-Din, who had formerly held the position.

With the exception of Saeed Ahmed in the second innings, Alim alone stood up to the English bowling with any degree of confidence. Three wickets fell for 73 by the close of play on the second day and on the third day the remaining seventeen wickets fell to the England bowlers in a most inept display of batting. Alim was top scorer in both innings, with 50 in the first and 60 in the second innings, and only Saeed with 54 in the second innings offered him any solid support. Pakistan's first innings effort of 131 all out was bettered only by 50 runs in the second innings and overall they did not offer a challenge to the England bowling and by losing the match the series went to England in three straight games.

The bowling was competent without being spectacular and the wickets were divided evenly among five players. In the match as a whole Statham took six wickets, Dexter five, Trueman four, Allen three and Titmus two. It was a workmanlike performance by all of the England bowlers which was far superior to anything offered back by the Pakistanis and doubts arise, because of three heavy defeats, of the effectiveness of the tourists' play in 1962.

The series continued with the Fourth Test, at Trent Bridge, and Pakistan found some small consolation in that they managed to escape with a draw. 'Escape' is the correct description for had the weather been kinder and had England held their chances on the final day the result would undoubtedly have been in the home side's favour. Burki again won the toss and for the second time in succession asked England to bat but before a ball could be bowled the heavens opened and play was washed out for the day.

Play began on time on the second morning and Pakistan gained instant success when Pullar fell leg before with the score on 11. The joy was short-lived as two large partnerships followed immediately; Dexter and Sheppard combined to add 161 runs for the second wicket followed by a stand of 184 runs between Graveney and Parfitt for the fourth wicket. The latter pair were the tormentors-in-chief of the tourists throughout the summer of 1962 and it was rubbing salt in the wound that they should be together when both compiling yet another century apiece off the bewildered Pakistan attack. For Graveney, his 114 was his fourth century of the tour against Pakistan, while for Parfitt his score of 101 not out had an added significance. Prior to the Test Match Parfitt had scored two centuries in the same match when playing for his county against the tourists and his effort at Trent Bridge gave him three centuries in successive innings, a most remarkable achievement. In all, Parfitt had scored six centuries out of seven innings against the Pakistanis, counting one century in Karachi on the winter tour of 1961–2, a feat without parallel in the history of Tests between the two countries. Such was Parfitt's superiority over the Pakistani bowling in 1962 that he, at one stage, had shared in no less than five separate record-breaking partnerships; namely for the fourth, sixth, seventh, eighth and tenth wickets. Records can always be broken but to hold so many at one time shows a remarkable degree of consistency and it is little wonder that Parfitt is able to speak of the 1962 Pakistanis with such conviction, as has been seen earlier in the chapter. Neither is it benign respect when noting that during his career Parfitt played against every Test-playing country in an official Test, thus giving him every opportunity to realise the strength of the opposition he was playing against at the time.

As for the Trent Bridge Test, Dexter declared as soon as Parfitt completed his century. Pakistan were in immediate trouble, losing Hanif off the second ball of the innings to Trueman and wickets fell steadily throughout the third day. At the close six wickets were down for 127 runs and apart from spirited resistance by Nasim-Ul-Ghani the remaining wickets soon capitulated on the fourth morning. The tourists were forced to follow on 209 runs behind and although they batted better in the second innings England should have completed a comfortable victory. The turning point came when an hour's play remained on the last day. At that stage a draw appeared to be the obvious outcome but Trueman suddenly had two catches dropped off his bowling in the same over which could have swung the game England's way. Mushtaq, then 80 not out, was dropped by the substitute and Shahid was dropped by Titmus at first slip before scoring. Had either chance, if not both, gone to hand, the result could well have been in the balance. Neither chance was held and in securing a draw for his side Mushtaq went on to complete his second Test century and in doing so became the first batsman in history to score two Test centuries before reaching the age of twenty.

The result was a draw but Trueman could rest at ease. The Fourth Test gave him another five wickets (4 for 71 and 1 for 35), taking his total for the series to twenty-two. He was not picked for the final Test at the Oval, where England made six changes to assist the teams involved in the County Championship, but his total from the first four Tests was enough to make Trueman the leading English wicket-taker for the sixth time in his career in a series and take his overall total on to 216.

The next objective for Trueman was Alec Bedser's world record of 236 Test wickets but he was not alone in his quest. Brian Statham also had his sights firmly fixed on the record and, at this stage, had a sizeable lead over Trueman. At the end of the Pakistan series Statham's total had reached 229, only seven behind the record, while Trueman was another thirteen wickets adrift. Both players were selected for the winter tour to Australia and there would be an interesting duel between the pair to see who would reach the goal first but with his sizeable lead Statham had to be a firm favourite to attain the glory first. He did, but Trueman was to run him perilously close before the vital wicket came and then it would only be a matter of weeks before he claimed the record for himself.

AVERAGES FOR 1962 SERIES *v* PAKISTAN: Five Tests, Played Four

Overs	*Mdns*	*Runs*	*Wkts*	*Ave*
164.5	37	439	22	19.69

Inns	*NO*	*Runs*	*HS*	*Ave*
2	0	49	29	24.50

Catches=6

Match results=England 4, Pakistan 0, 1 Match drawn.

Statistics
1 Total Test wickets=216
2 Total catches=50
3 Total runs= 695
4 Total appearances=49

12 Australia and New Zealand, on tour, 1962/3

The 1962–3 tour to Australia was Trueman's fourth overseas trip with MCC and it transpired to be his last. Similar to events that had occurred so often in the past the tour did not pass without a touch of rancour creeping into the affair for some of the participants and, as usual, the blame lay on MCC's own doorstep. Not for the first time did MCC choose a controversial manager. On the other hand, the decision to give the job to the Duke of Norfolk was a diplomatic success. He would be a most welcome guest at the inevitable cocktail parties and luncheons to be attended on the tour but those functions bore little relation to the efforts of men on the field of play.

The England players were in Australia to win back the Ashes, a very tough proposition under any circumstances, but one made infinitely harder when the manager was sitting on an aristocratic pedestal far out of the reach of the majority of the team. There were other more suitable candidates but a significant factor, totally unconnected with cricket, was that shortly after the cricket tour Her Majesty the Queen was making a visit to Australia. Since it was the Duke of Norfolk who organised such Royal events it does not need much imagination to realise why the Duke went on the tour as manager.

A manager's duties are many and varied: ensuring the smooth day-to-day running of the team; press conferences; player's individual problems and many other facets are all part and parcel of the job. With a man such as the Duke of Norfolk in charge it would not be easy to readjust to this new form of leadership and at one stage of the tour it was impossible simply because the Duke returned to London on business. The length of time spent away is immaterial. The fact that the team was left to run its own affairs, no matter how able the deputies, left much to be desired in the ways of wise management from the men at the top. Cricket apart, the appointment was an unqualified success, especially among the social elite and one of the prime questions asked was whether or not the Duke's racing colours would be seen in Australia. How a horse or jockey can help to win the Ashes is beyond comprehension but MCC obviously thought the whole charade was the right prescription to give the team for the duration of an arduous tour.

The party was captained by Ted Dexter who on his day could be one of the most exciting attacking batsmen in the world. His elegant, precision-like, forceful strokeplay was a delight to watch but captaincy was a different matter. On paper, Dexter's team appeared to have a reasonable chance of regaining the Ashes, and, no matter what the outcome, they certainly could not fare worse than Peter May's team of 1958–9 when his side was trounced four-nil.

One possible pointer in England's favour was that the Australians were reaching the end of an era. Benaud, Harvey and Davidson were all on the verge of retirement, making a transitional rebuilding stage unavoidable for the team and England were in a position to take advantage of this. This did occur when a one-nil lead was taken in the series but this was needlessly thrown away by strange decisions on the part of the selectors and captain. Criticism is an occupational hazard of the men who pick teams but there is little doubt that their curious twists of fancy were to cost the side dearly by the end of the Fifth Test. No less absolved from blame was Dexter. Tactics were not his strong point and in the First Test there was a definite chance of victory but a safety-first attitude prevailed that decreed England should bat out time instead.

The series commenced at Brisbane where the last Test Match to be played there had produced the historic tied game between Australia and West Indies and it would need some very exciting cricket to follow such an entertaining match as that had been two years earlier. Benaud won the toss and on a pitch which promised some early assistance to the bowlers decided to bat. England, and Trueman in particular, met with immediate success. By lunch the Australians were 97 for 3 and shortly afterwards 101 for 4 with Trueman having claimed three of the wickets to fall. There was some life and lift in the pitch which

Trueman exploited with sustained vigour and in an inspired piece of bowling dismissed Lawry, O'Neill and Burge for just 29 runs. Those figures are a truer indication of his bowling and put into a clearer perspective his final analysis of 18–0–76–3 for Trueman bowled much better than the figures would indicate.

England maintained a strong grip on the game, taking another wicket to have half the Australian side back in the pavilion for 140 runs. Slowly, the home team rallied to wrest the initiative back in their favour and finally the Australians totalled 404 all out, an extremely good effort after the poor start to the innings. Trueman added to his wickets by taking two catches, one of which was a particularly fine piece of fielding. Davidson swept Barrington hard and high towards the backward square-leg boundary. Trueman took the ball, chest high and pressed hard against the fence to save a certain six and make a brilliant catch at the same time.

England did not fare too badly when batting but narrowly failed to take a first innings lead by 15. The most notable incident in the innings came when Trueman was dismissed for 19, caught behind off McKenzie. He batted with typical brashness, striking the ball hard in an effort to take his side into the lead and when he was at last out the decision did not please Trueman at all. He thought the ball hit his hip rather than his bat and for the trouble Trueman took to remonstrate about the decision he was made to apologise to umpire Wykis. This was made public before play began on the following day when the Duke of Norfolk read a statement to that effect. Once again Trueman had been humiliated by the authorities.

By the end of the fourth day's play Australia had set England a target of just over 380 runs. There was a full day in which to reach the target and this meant, in terms of runs per minute, a striking rate of 63 per hour. It gave both sides a chance of victory, with Australia holding a slight edge in favour, but given a good start England had the batsmen with which to deliver a challenge. The side did get off to a very good start and while a continuous scoring rate of 63 an hour all day was a stiff proposition the foundation was laid for an attack to be launched on the Australian bowlers.

The England openers, Pullar and Sheppard, made 114 before

being parted. This could have provided the springboard to victory but the first 80 of those runs took up the whole of the morning session leaving England to score at 150 a session in the remaining two periods of play to force a win. A little more adventurous play in the early stages would have reduced this target considerably but defence was more in favour than attack. England never really entertained the idea of going for victory and the final score was 278 for 6, with the side in no danger of losing which was exactly what the team had set out to accomplish.

While a rather tame draw was not the ideal result to set English hearts fluttering there had been several plus signs in England's team performance. The openers had batted very well in the second innings while Trueman had been very hostile in his first spell and also there was the batting display by Peter Parfitt. He had only recently established himself in the side and scored 80 in England's first innings but nevertheless was promptly dropped for the Second Test at Melbourne.

Parfitt had been under some pressure in that he was preferred to the more experienced Tom Graveney when the side was chosen for the First Test. Unperturbed, the Middlesex left-hander put together an excellent innings of 80 in his first appearance against Australia. The decision to drop him for the Second Test seems inexplicable. The Brisbane Test was Parfitt's tenth appearance in all for England during which time he had rattled up a very impressive average and scored four centuries in the process. He played his first Test at Bombay on the 1961–2 tour to India and Pakistan and his first century, 111, came against the latter country later in the same tour. On returning to England, Parfitt took runs galore off the 1962 Pakistan tourists to finish that series with an average of 113.33 and he became an automatic choice for the Australian tour. At that time his impressive credentials read as follows:

Tests	*Inns*	*NO*	*Runs*	*HS*	*Ave*
9	11	2	585	119	65.00

Following on from this earlier success came Parfitt's fine Brisbane performance which more than maintained his Test Match average but it all counted for nothing. Graveney returned to the team in his place and Parfitt went on to play in only one more Test, the Third, in Australia that winter though he did break a finger halfway through the tour.

Melbourne, venue for the Second Test, provided England with their one Test victory of the tour. The result was a handsome seven-wicket triumph and by taking a one-nil lead in the series England became instant favourites to regain the Ashes. Australia batted first on a good pitch when Benaud won the toss and at lunch on the first day were comfortably placed at 93 for 1. The position altered dramatically shortly afterwards when three wickets fell for one run and although the Australians battled hard they never recovered completely from this blow. The close of play score was 263 for 7, which gave England a fair measure of success after losing the toss and having to bowl on a good batting track.

The innings was concluded on the second day at 316 all out of which Trueman's share of the spoils was 3 for 83. They were far from being his most impressive figures but they were obtained off twenty-three overs that were bowled in gruelling heat and they were a foretaste of much better things to come in the second innings.

Cowdrey was in excellent form when England batted and mainly by his century a first innings lead was secured. Ironically, it was by the same margin of runs that had been in Australia's favour at the same stage of the game in the First Test. By a strange coincidence the same figures often recur in Test Match records. Trueman's match tally of wickets corresponded exactly on numerous occasions with England's wicket-victory margin in certain Tests and a similar type of occurrence took place at Melbourne when England gained a 15-run lead on the first innings. The state of play was very evenly balanced with so little between the two sides but Trueman was soon in the action to catapult England towards a victory.

The Australian second innings score stood at 30 for 0 when Trueman produced his electrifying two-ball burst which swung the game England's way. Simpson went first, receiving a perfect delivery which sent his off-stump reeling and seconds later O'Neill was departing from the crease, brilliantly caught by

Cowdrey in the slips diving away to his right. The gods never favoured Trueman when a hat-trick was in prospect but the two wickets were enough to place England in a wonderful position. The Australians had had the ground taken from underneath their feet by Trueman and apart from a resilient, gritty century by Booth the home side did not regain the initiative. The innings closed at 248 all out with Trueman's final return being the very respectable figures of 20–1–62–5 and they were his best return from any of his eight Test appearances on Australian soil.

England required 234 to win. The runs were accumulated with ease, only three wickets falling in the second innings, and with another century, this time by Sheppard, England clinched an emphatic win. It had been a splendid performance by England, especially from Trueman whose long stint of bowling in the second innings had been under a blazing sun, and with the batsmen playing their part too, the Ashes were in sight. One game to the good with three left to play placed England firmly in command and the Ashes ought to have been homeward bound at the end of the tour but in the very next Test England, or more particularly the selectors, threw the Ashes back to the Australians.

The Third Test was to be played at Sydney, a ground where, on assorted previous occasions, the wicket had favoured the faster bowlers. This custom did not prevail in 1963 and England's selectors paid dearly for their choice of three seam bowlers, instead of picking an extra spinner. Yet, incredibly, there was a general consensus of opinion before the game started that the wicket would take spin! The batting strip was totally devoid of grass but it was still decided to play the full complement of pace bowlers comprising Trueman, Statham and Coldwell rather than risk having two spinners in the side. Apart from Titmus, who played in the match, England had two other competent exponents of off-spin available in Illingworth and Allen and from the sequence of events during the game it is more than likely that had either played England would have gone two-up in the series.

The net result of all the deliberations was an eight-wicket win by Australia who thereby levelled the series at one game each.

The whole question of whether or not the extra spinner should have been chosen was conclusively resolved in the Australian first innings but that came after England had taken first strike. Dexter won the toss for the first time in the series but the success was muted when England were dismissed for a rather moderate score of 279 all out.

Australia overhauled the score to take a first innings lead of some 40 runs but throughout their innings they were tormented by Titmus. In his spell of twenty-seven overs he was accuracy personified. With one more recognised finger-spinner in the team Australia would have faced serious difficulties but with nobody to supplement Titmus' efforts the game slipped away from England. Ironically, there were two players on the field with a knowledge of spin-bowling, Barrington and Parfitt, and though neither would claim to be in the Titmus class, there were possibilities in their presence being utilised. Unfortunately, the one most likely to have aided Titmus the more substantially, Parfitt, was engaged early in the innings as a deputy for wicket-keeper Murray who had to leave the field.

Barrington could, and did on occasions, bowl effective leg-breaks in Test cricket but Parfitt, more importantly, was a genuine off-spinner in the same mould as Titmus. However, Murray tore ligaments in his shoulder early in the innings when taking a spectacular diving catch down the leg-side to dismiss Lawry off Coldwell and Parfitt was the chosen deputy for his county colleague. This left Titmus to trundle away on his own and with necessity being the mother of invention perhaps Parfitt would have been more gainfully employed with his finger-spin rather than wearing the wicket-keeper's gloves. With no other alternative it was worth at least a try but as it did not materialise it must be left in the realms of conjecture. Titmus' final figures prove how much England needed the extra spinner. They read: 27–14–79–7, it was a brilliant and outstanding example of slow bowling that ranks amongst Titmus' finest performances for England.

For Trueman, the match was a disappointing follow-up to his efforts at Melbourne but on a wicket so ideally suited to spin bowling this was not surprising. From both innings Trueman managed only two wickets for 88 runs and both came in the

Trueman's 300th Test wicket. Neil Hawke (Australia) is caught in the slips by Colin Cowdrey during the fifth Test at the Oval, 1964.

Fred Trueman, 1966.

second innings as Australia strolled to an eight-wicket win. They had won as easily at Sydney as England had in the Second Test; all the selectors could do was look back and ponder on what might have transpired if only they had . . . If only. Two small words with such large consequences.

Retrospective thinking came to the fore when the series moved on to Adelaide for the Fourth Test. There, on a pitch begging for a full pace attack, the selectors completely reversed their Sydney decision and dropped Coldwell in favour of Illingworth. Trueman emphasised the state of the wicket by taking 4 for 60 off 23.3 overs in the Australian second innings but by then it was too late to be of any advantage. A draw became Benaud's prime objective from the early stages of England's first innings (Australia batted first) when Davidson tore a hamstring muscle. He took no further part in the game and without this vital attacking force at his disposal Benaud was in no position to offer England anything resembling a generous target. Benaud immediately went on to the defensive and from the moment of Davidson's injury the game was destined to be a draw.

While the Adelaide Test was relatively tame in terms of cricket, excitement of a different nature came from another quarter. Alec Bedser's long-standing world record of 236 Test wickets was finally passed, not by Trueman but by John Brian Statham. The record had been the target of both men for a considerable time and it was a fitting coincidence that they should combine their talents to create the new record. Trueman held the catch to dismiss Shepherd which gave Statham the hard-earned title. Trueman could count himself a shade unlucky not to have reached the goal first: Statham's Test career had commenced nearly two years before Trueman gained his first appearance and by the time Statham took the record Trueman was only a handful of wickets behind his Lancastrian counterpart. At the end of the Adelaide Test Trueman's total number of wickets was 234, a mere two behind the old record but the most important point is that it was Statham who did break the record and not Trueman. It was a well-deserved accolade for Statham. During the years he had been a member of the England team he had given wonderful unstinting service to his side and the record came as a result of much hard work and a great deal of skill.

When the teams returned to Sydney for the final Test there appeared to be everything to play for between the two sides. A win for either side would clinch the series and the Ashes, while a draw would suffice Australian requirements but there was only one conclusive winner at the end of the five days—the pitch. Australia introduced a new pace bowler to Test cricket in the shape of Neil Hawke, a twenty-three year old who played for South Australia, and as so often happens when a player makes his international debut the memory stayed firmly implanted in his memory long after the last ball had been bowled. Somewhat surprisingly that memory is limited to one brief sentence but the vivid thought came without hesitation, 'It was the slowest pitch I ever played a Test Match on,' he said, and that provides a simple solution to a dull, lifeless, drawn game.

A measure of how very true Hawke's words were came when England batted in their first innings. Trueman occupied the crease for one hour fifty minutes, making his best-ever Test score of 38 against Australia, yet in that time he did not hit one boundary. That was a strange occurrence indeed from a man who was never noted for any preoccupation with defence when batting! Neil Hawke, of course, was to figure much more prominently in Trueman's career, some two years hence, than the timid cricket at Sydney had allowed but, for the time being, this 1962–3 series had drawn to a close. Sadly, for England, the Ashes had not been regained despite taking a one-nil lead. The series ended all-square at one win apiece, with three games drawn and all that remained was the short end-of-tour visit to New Zealand before making the long journey home.

The four months in Australia had been a time of mixed fortunes for Trueman. The tour was one of the very rare occasions in his career when his physical fitness appeared to be in doubt and at one stage he was in grave danger of breaking down completely. All of the top-line fast bowlers, who were on the scene several years or more (ie Statham, Hall, Davidson, Lindwall, Miller, etc) had to be superb athletes and this was no less true of Trueman. He was a fine all-round sportsman but at Brisbane he developed a mysterious back ailment. Exactly the same thing had occurred, at the same time and place, on the 1958–9 tour but on this second occasion the complaint appeared to be far more serious and there was even talk of him having to return home. Fortunately, Trueman recovered and was able to carry on for the rest of the tour, including the New Zealand part.

A remarkable aspect of Trueman's position as premier bowler in the side and his possible breakdown was the unduly heavy work-load he was given on the tour. He took part in more than two-thirds of the up-country and state games in addition to playing in all five Tests. Fast bowlers are not workhorses who thrive on a continual diet of bowling. They need rest occasionally yet rarely was this granted to Trueman. A direct consequence of this repeated selection in Australia came when the team moved on to New Zealand (minus Statham who had gone straight home) was that they had to play the First Test without Trueman—ironically, he was suffering from leg-strain.

AVERAGES FOR 1962–3 SERIES *v* AUSTRALIA: Five Tests, Played Five

Overs	*Mdns*	*Runs*	*Wkts*	*Ave*
158.3	9	521	20	26.05

Inns	*NO*	*Runs*	*HS*	*Ave*
7	0	142	38	20.28

Catches=7

Match results=Australia 1, England 1, 3 Matches drawn.

Statistics
1 Total Test wickets=236
2 Total catches=57
3 Total runs=837
4 Total appearances=54

N.B. This was the first and only occasion Trueman scored over 100 runs in a Test series.

The MCC team moved on to New Zealand to complete the

final leg of the tour where there were three Tests to be played on a four-match agenda. They gave Trueman the instant opportunity to capture the world record total of Test wickets just weeks after Statham had set the new record in Adelaide. The Lancashire favourite did not go to New Zealand, leaving the stage to Trueman but the record did not finally fall into his grasp until the very last match of the tour. Statham's total stood at 242 compared to Trueman's 236 when the three-match series began in New Zealand, an insignificant difference, but Trueman encountered an immediate hurdle because he was forced to miss the First Test at Auckland. He was suffering from leg-strain and it was not until the Second Test at Wellington began that Trueman could commence his quest for the seven wickets that would wrest the crown away from Statham.

At Wellington, Trueman made rapid inroads against the rather weak New Zealand batting when the New Zealanders took first strike. Out of a total of 194 all out Trueman collected 4 for 46 off twenty overs and with the aid of an undefeated century from Cowdrey this score was passed with ease by England. Dexter declared at 428 for 8, setting the New Zealanders a target of 234 to avoid an innings defeat and although Trueman could add only one wicket to his total in the New Zealand second innings England still gained a very comfortable victory by an innings and 47 runs.

The five wickets gleaned by Trueman from the Second Test placed him just one behind Statham. Everything depended upon the last Test of the tour and Trueman made certain he broke the record in style. The Third Test was played at Christchurch, the same ground where four years earlier Trueman had reached his first major milestone by taking his 100th wicket in Test cricket. Now, he would not only beat the existing world record but hoist the figure to an incredible 250. Thus, eleven years after his career began Trueman's name could be placed in the record books against a record that belonged entirely to him. The road had been long but the Christchurch game made it all worthwhile.

New Zealand batted first but none of their batsmen could properly master Trueman. Systematically, he worked his way through the batting to take seven wickets, the second highest number of wickets he was to claim in a single Test innings in his entire career. It was a well-earned success rather than a short spectacular burst, coming off 30.2 overs and only against India in 1952 had Trueman taken more wickets in an innings in a Test Match. The scorecard read as follows:

NEW ZEALAND *v* ENGLAND: THIRD TEST MATCH AT CHRISTCHURCH 15, 16, 18, 19 MARCH 1963

NEW ZEALAND: 1ST INNINGS

G. T. Dowling	c Dexter	b Titmus	40
W. R. Playle	c Barrington	b Trueman	0
B. W. Sinclair	hit wicket	b Trueman	44
J. R. Reid	c Parfitt	b Knight	74
P. T. Barton	c Smith	b Knight	11
M. J. Shrimpton	c Knight	b Trueman	31
A. E. Dick		b Trueman	16
R. C. Motz	c Parfitt	b Trueman	7
R. W. Blair	c Parfitt	b Trueman	0
J. C. Alabaster	not out		20
F. J. Cameron	c Smith	b Trueman	1
	Extras	b 1 lb 9 w 3 nb 9	22
			266

FALL OF WICKETS

1	*2*	*3*	*4*	*5*	*6*	*7*	*8*	*9*
3	83	98	127	195	234	235	235	262

BOWLING	*O*	*M*	*R*	*W*
Trueman	30.2	9	75	7
Larter	21	5	59	0
Knight	23	5	39	2
Titmus	30	13	45	1
Dexter	9	3	8	0
Barrington	5	0	18	0

Trueman's follow-up display in the New Zealanders' second innings (on which they held a slight lead of 13 runs over England's first attempt of 253 all out) was not as impressive in terms of numbers of wickets but of the two he did take, the second one was unique.

J. C. Alabaster c Parfitt b Trueman 1

That succinct entry meant Trueman was the first man ever to take 250 Test wickets and Trueman could return home from the tour well contented with his labours. The tour had experienced several rough patches but throughout the seven Tests in which he played, Trueman's consistency never wavered. Thirty-four wickets was a fine reward for five months' hard work and he was the undisputed leader of the pack now that the record belonged to him alone. The next target on the horizon was the triple century, a figure previously not thought to be possible until Trueman arrived on the scene. Yet, Trueman himself would not expect the 300 figure to quite as close as it would be by the end of the 1963 home series against West Indies. What he had accomplished in the seven Tests in the winter (ie taken thirty-four Test wickets) he was to emulate in the West Indies series in just five Tests. Even by his own remarkable standards 1963 was to be a fantastic summer for Trueman.

AVERAGES FOR 1962–3 SERIES *v* NEW ZEALAND: Three Tests, Played Two

Overs	*Mdns*	*Runs*	*Wkts*	*Ave*
88	29	164	14	11.71

Inns	*NO*	*Runs*	*HS*	*Ave*
2	0	14	11	7.00

Catches=0

Match results=New Zealand 0, England 3.

Statistics
1 Total Test wickets=250
2 Total catches=57
3 Total runs=851
4 Total appearances=56

13 West Indies, at home, 1963

There was no Test Match respite for Trueman after the exacting winter tour of Australia and New Zealand. Close though he had been to breaking down on that tour Trueman's fitness was never questioned in the summer of 1963 and he took part in the full five-match series played against the West Indian tourists. The talented Caribbean cricketers were undertaking their sixth visit to England since tours began in 1928 and they were a very popular side, drawing large, vocal crowds wherever they played.

The West Indians were recognised as a very strong side, far stronger than the previous team to visit England six years previously. Three years earlier West Indies had gone to Australia and their calypso cricketers had won considerable acclaim. The tour had aroused the public interest in a way not imagined prior to the series commencing, and the climax had been the unique Tied Test at Brisbane. The series against Australia established West Indies as a definite power in world cricket and the 1963 series, in view of England's extremely good track record at home over the years, was clearly going to be a very hard fought affair. The West Indies squad had immense all-round ability and England would find it was no easy task facing their battery of fast bowlers, glorious strokemakers and sparkling fielders.

Many of the tourists had already played a good deal of cricket in England, which availed the players with valuable experience of the conditions, climatic and otherwise, they were likely to encounter in the series. Nine players had held professional league appointments while five of the squad had previously toured England with John Goddard's team in 1957. The no less capable Frank Worrell was in charge of the 1963 team but his task was simplified to a large extent because he had an almost perfect side to lead. The attack possessed three extremely fast bowlers in Hall, Griffith and King with the dependable Gibbs spearheading the spin bowling with his customary effortless ease. All-round support came from Sobers and Worrell and when this pair was added to a batting line-up which included Hunte, McMorris, Kanhai and Carew, amongst others, it was patently obvious that this was a side to give England a very stern test indeed in the forthcoming series.

A new trophy was at stake in the series, presented by the proprietors of *Wisden*, and it was known simply as the Wisden Trophy. It was to be competed for on similar lines to the Ashes (ie in every series between the two countries) and by the end of August West Indies had accomplished their task. The inaugural contesting of the Wisden Trophy had gone their way, after a most exciting series, by three games to one, with one match drawn. It was a brilliant all-round performance by an outstanding team and the scoreline emulated exactly the success of the very good West Indies side of 1950, which was the last time the tourists had won a rubber in England.

The series got off to a flying start for the tourists, with a crushing victory in the very First Test, played at Old Trafford. The main reason for England's humiliating defeat was the mammoth total West Indies accumulated in their first innings, 501 for 6 declared. It was a daunting prospect for any side to face up to while contemplating the possibility of also having to bat fourth whatever score might be made in the first innings and as a result the match was virtually settled by the West Indian first innings total. A remarkable fact to emerge from such a huge total was that only one century was scored by the visiting batsmen. It went to opener Conrad Hunte, who scored 182 quite brilliant runs, although Kanhai should have been another to reach the goal. He needlessly ran himself out when 90 by dashing down the wicket after hitting the ball straight to Allen at mid-on. Hunte stayed his ground, leaving the rather reckless Kanhai hopelessly stranded and thereby paying the highest price for his folly. Such characteristics were a hallmark of Kanhai's play, however, and when in full flight he was glorious, an unorthodox strokemaker of the highest calibre.

Throughout the tourists' innings, Trueman bowled through forty stamina-sapping overs. His reward was a meagre 2 for 95 but the figures belie the zest and enthusiasm he put into his work and away from the cold light protracted by the bare figures this was a creditable performance. While taking only two wickets Trueman proved his worth by giving away little more than 2 runs an over and it was one more plus sign in his all-round ability. It is one thing to bowl well and look a world beater on a pitch which helps the bowler but quite another to bowl with sustained vigour on a wicket which gives no assistance whatsoever and that is precisely what Trueman achieved in the West Indies first innings at Old Trafford.

As the England first innings progressed it became increasingly obvious that the pitch was taking spin. Gibbs was particularly effective, claiming 5 for 57, out of an English total of 205 all out and Dexter, in an innings of 73, was the only batsman to offer prolonged resistance. Worrell needed no second bidding to enforce the follow-on. England required 296 runs to avoid an innings defeat and when the ninth wicket fell at 268 that derisory demise appeared imminent but Trueman was in no mood to allow such an inglorious conclusion to the game. Putting bat to ball with venomous force he smote both Gibbs and Sobers for towering sixes. Statham did likewise to Gibbs and at this Worrell recalled Griffith to the attack. The West Indian paceman summarily concluded the innings by bowling the left-handed number eleven but not before the scores had drawn level. West Indies would have to bat again to score the one run required for victory.

The swashbuckling efforts of Trueman and Statham had staved off the ignominy of an innings defeat, albeit by a hair's breadth. Trueman's share, 29 not out, was his highest score of the series but it was of little real worth apart from sparing England a few blushes. Not that a ten-wicket hammering was any worse than an innings defeat. West Indies duly won the match off the only ball bowled in their second innings, sent down by Allen but, on the lighter side, the solitary delivery did give him a rare claim to fame. It was very seldom, if ever, that an off-spinner could say in all honesty he had opened the bowling for England in a Test Match. Not even Laker had done that when he took nineteen wickets against Australia on the same ground in 1956!

The Second Test, played at Lord's, was a stupendous affair

and was one of the most dramatic Tests ever played in England. In some ways the game went as far as to match the unique Tie played by the same West Indians at Brisbane in 1960. The suspense, courage and climax the game produced was enthralling and made a riveting spectacle for those fortunate enough to be present. The cricket was thrilling throughout the match but the finale was truly remarkable, more akin to fantasy than to real-life drama and the twenty-two participants gave a wonderful advertisement to the game's spectator appeal. Not least of these was Colin Cowdrey. When he had to go to the wicket in England's second innings, with his arm in plaster, and only two deliveries remaining in the match there were no less than four possible results hanging in the balance. And that is every single result available to any two sides engaged in a game of cricket!

Early in the England second innings Cowdrey had received a nasty, lifting ball from Hall which, after impact with Cowdrey's left arm, resulted in a broken bone. Consequently, when the ninth English wicket fell it was imperative that Cowdrey went to the crease in order to save the game for England. But that was not all. When Cowdrey joined David Allen in the middle England required just 6 runs to win from the remaining two balls of Hall's final over of the match. Fortunately, Cowdrey was not going in to face the bowling. The ninth wicket had fallen to a run-out and with one arm in plaster it is incomprehensible to think of Cowdrey facing even one delivery. Allen took the one sensible option open to him and calmly played the last two deliveries back down the pitch without attempting to go for victory. It was by far the wisest decision. Six runs off two deliveries was easily attainable, especially with a tightly set, close-in field but it would have been foolhardy in the extreme to have risked Cowdrey having to face the last ball. Such a move would have placed both batsman and bowler in an intolerable position, therefore a draw was a worthy result for both sides after an outstanding game of cricket. In conclusion, for the uninitiated, the four results available when Cowdrey went out to bat with two deliveries left were: an England win, a West Indies win, a Draw or a Tie.

On a different plane, the match was personal triumph for Trueman. In the two West Indies innings, he claimed match figures of 11 for 152 and the performance ranked alongside the best of his career for England. At the start of the game this would have appeared a nonsensical proposition. The first three deliveries of his first over were dispatched to the boundary with consummate ease by Hunte but, undaunted by this show of aggression, Trueman stuck to his task manfully. Revenge came when he dismissed both openers and Trueman went on to claim four more wickets in a very long stint of bowling. Altogether in the first innings Trueman powered his way through forty-four overs, four more than in the corresponding innings of the First Test, but the reward for his toil was substantial and he finished with 6 wickets for 100 runs.

Trueman continued his excellent form in the West Indies second innings. On the morning of the fourth day the tourists were seemingly well placed with a lead of 218 runs and five wickets still intact. In a shattering spell lasting a mere twenty-five minutes Trueman, partnered by Shackleton, ripped this advantage away from West Indies. In just six overs the five wickets went down for the addition of 15 and Trueman completed an excellent match with Figures of 5 for 52. His total of eleven wickets was equal to his previous best in a Test and was the second time in his eleven-year career that he had reached double figures in a Test. The full West Indian scorecard read as follows:

ENGLAND *v* WEST INDIES: SECOND TEST AT LORD'S 20, 21, 22, 24, 25 JUNE 1963

WEST INDIES:	1ST INNINGS			2ND INNINGS		
C. C. Hunte	c Close	b Trueman	44	c Cowdrey	b Shackleton	7
E. D. McMorris	lbw	b Trueman	16	c Cowdrey	b Trueman	8
G. S. Sobers	c Cowdrey	b Allen	42	c Parks	b Trueman	8
R. B. Kanhai	c Edrich	b Trueman	73	c Cowdrey	b Shackleton	21
B. F. Butcher	c Barrington	b Trueman	14	lbw	b Shackleton	133
J. S. Soloman	lbw	b Shackleton	56	c Stewart	b Allen	5
F. M. Worrell		b Trueman	0	c Stewart	b Trueman	33
D. L. Murray	c Cowdrey	b Trueman	20	c Parks	b Trueman	2
W. W. Hall	not out		25	c Parks	b Trueman	2
C. C. Griffith	c Cowdrey	b Shackleton	0		b Shackleton	1

L. R. Gibbs	c Stewart	b Shackleton	0	not out		1
	Extras	b 10 lb 1	11	Extras	b 5 lb 2 nb 1	8
			301			229

FALL OF WICKETS

1st Innings

1	*2*	*3*	*4*	*5*	*6*	*7*	*8*	*9*
51	64	127	145	219	219	263	297	297

2nd Innings

1	*2*	*3*	*4*	*5*	*6*	*7*	*8*	*9*
15	15	64	84	104	214	224	226	228

BOWLING	*O*	*M*	*R*	*W*	*O*	*M*	*R*	*W*
Trueman	44	16	100	6	26	9	52	5
Shackleton	50.2	22	93	3	34	14	72	4
Dexter	20	6	41	0				
Close	9	3	21	0				
Allen	10	3	35	1	21	7	50	1
Titmus					17	3	47	0

Trueman's prowess was showing few signs of weakening and he demonstrated this perfectly in the next match, the third of the series, at Edgbaston where he performed even better than at Lord's. Yet to lose a Test at the Warwickshire ground, England maintained the record in fine style with a 217 run victory but it was brought about entirely by Trueman's one-man demolition show which paralysed the West Indies second innings and this came after a praiseworthy effort in the first innings.

Rain badly interfered with play while the game was in progress and Trueman varied his tactics accordingly. The fourth day was the first full day's play but prior to that Trueman had given notice of his continued good form. He reduced his speed and resorted to bowling cutters, making far greater use of the seam, and the ploy was admirably successful. Five wickets went his way for 75 runs but this was nothing compared to the devastating spell he produced when West Indies batted a second time. The scene was set on the last day when Dexter declared England's second innings closed at 278 for 9. The time was shortly after midday and in the four hours forty minutes left for play the tourists had to score 309 runs to win. This was a required scoring rate of 67 per hour, a high target but one well within the capabilities of the talented West Indies batsmen if they began to play their strokes. The possibility did not occur. England struck early and the advantage seized was not allowed to slip away.

Both West Indies openers were dismissed by the time 10 had been scored, a disastrous start from which the visitors could not recover. Carew went in Shackleton's first over followed shortly afterwards by Hunte, dismissed by Trueman, and after bowling for fifty minutes the latter was rested with the scoreboard reading 32 for 2. At this point it is worth noting Trueman's analysis for later comparison with his final return: 7–0–24–1. When Trueman came off, Dexter went on and bowled Butcher for 14 and at lunch England had a better than evens chance of victory with the West Indies score standing rather shakily at 58 for 3.

Kanhai and Sobers resumed after lunch and for a brief spell Kanhai appeared to be in a punishing mood but it was not to last. England required less than an hour to snap up the remaining seven wickets for the addition of a paltry 33 runs. England were the team but it was Trueman who was the destroyer. His devastating spell of bowling was nothing short of being single-handed annihilation of West Indies batting line-up and his figures of 7 for 44, coupled with his first innings 5 for 75, gave Trueman his finest Test analysis of his entire career: 12 for 119. The final onslaught was shattering even by Trueman's own volcanic standards. The last six wickets all went to him at the expense of a single scoring stroke, and that was a thick edge for four through the slips off number eleven Gibbs.

The complete innings lasted just four minutes over two hours. West Indies mastered 91 runs for their efforts and an exultant Trueman deservedly led the team from the pitch when the rout was complete. This feat at Edgbaston was comparable to all of Trueman's Herculean exploits of the past: his 8 for 31 against India in 1952, his 11 for 88 against Australia at Headingley in 1961 and his 7 for 75 against New Zealand early in 1963. There had been many other fine performances with not quite so many wickets to show for the amount of energy expounded but Trueman's 7 for 44 against West Indies at Edgbaston in 1963 must approach very close to being his best-ever representation with a cricket ball for England. Moreover, the analysis gave Trueman, in two consecutive Tests, the staggering total of twenty-three wickets. For a fast bowler that was an amazing number of wickets to plunder yet he did this at the age of thirty-two, when many alleged 'experts' were considering Trueman to be past his best. The notion was sheer rubbish. If Trueman was past his peak when he played so well against West Indies it is beyond comprehension to think what he would have achieved years earlier when he was banished from the team because those years were generally acknowledged as having been his prime years as a bowler. Yet, eight or nine years later, he was still a top-flight, world-class performer.

The scorecard for Trueman's phenomenal bowling in the Third Test reads as follows:

ENGLAND *v* WEST INDIES: THIRD TEST AT EDGBASTON 4, 5, 6, 8, 9 JULY 1963

WEST INDIES	1ST INNINGS			2ND INNINGS		
C. C. Hunte		b Trueman	18	c Barrington	b Trueman	5
M. C. Carew	c and b	Trueman	40	lbw	b Shackleton	1
R. B. Kanhai	c Lock	b Shackleton	32	c Lock	b Trueman	38
B. F. Butcher	lbw	b Dexter	15		b Dexter	14
J. S. Soloman	lbw	b Dexter	0	c Parks	b Trueman	14
G. S. Sobers		b Trueman	19	c Sharpe	b Shackleton	9
F. M. Worrell		b Dexter	1	c Parks	b Trueman	0
D. L. Murray	not out		20	c Parks	b Trueman	3
W. W. Hall	c Sharpe	b Dexter	28		b Trueman	0
C. C. Griffith	lbw	b Trueman	5	lbw	b Trueman	0
L. R. Gibbs		b Trueman	0	not out		4
	Extras	lb 7 w 1	8	Extras	lb 2 w 1	3
			186			91

FALL OF WICKETS

1st Innings

1	*2*	*3*	*4*	*5*	*6*	*7*	*8*	*9*
42	79	108	109	128	130	130	178	186

2nd Innings

1	*2*	*3*	*4*	*5*	*6*	*7*	*8*	*9*
2	10	38	64	78	80	86	86	86

BOWLING	*O*	*M*	*R*	*W*	*O*	*M*	*R*	*W*
Trueman	26	5	75	5	14.3	2	44	7
Shackleton	21	9	60	1	17	4	37	2
Dexter	20	5	38	4	3	1	7	1
Lock	2	1	5	0				

The Third Test brought Trueman's number of wickets for the series up to twenty-five and levelled the rubber at one-game all. The Fourth Test was played at Headingley, Trueman's local ground, but it was not a happy homecoming for the Yorkshireman. For the third time in the series Trueman had to pound his way through more than forty overs as West Indies amassed a large first innings total. At Leeds the final score was 397 all out and while Trueman's share of the wickets was a respectable four the debit of 117 runs against him off forty-six overs gives an indication of how hard Trueman was forced to work for his just reward.

The four wickets, which Trueman took in the first innings, pushed his total for the summer up to twenty-nine which equalled his previous best in a full series against India in 1952, which had a four-match rubber. The 1963 series was spread over five Tests and as Trueman reached the twenty-nine mark in the Fourth Test (and passed it when he claimed two more wickets in the tourists' second innings) the performance could be rated as being better than his explosive exploits eleven years earlier. The difference in class between the two sides in opposition was akin to the gulf between the First Division and the Fourth Division of the Football League and meritorious though the 1952 achievements had been, the 1963 series gave a far richer indication of Trueman's bowling prowess.

England's batting performance in the first innings at Headingley was abysmal. The team was shot out for only 174 runs and but for a splendid, defiant half century by number ten Lock this would have been considerably less. Worrell declined to enforce the follow-on, a rather surprising tactic when in such a commanding position, but the manoeuvre certainly eliminated any remote possibility of defeat. The lead was extended to

453 runs by the time the second innings was concluded and England's only hope of saving the game was to pray for some form of divine intervention. None was forthcoming. The England batting was a little better at the second attempt but, shortly after lunch on the fourth day, West Indies snapped up the tenth English wicket to complete a resounding 221 run success and by it edge two-one ahead in the series.

Trueman's sole consolation was that his total of wickets for the series was now over thirty. Six wickets in the match gave him thirty-one altogether for the four Tests and with one more still to be played it was not inconceivable that the extremely rare figure of forty could have been reached. It was a tall order, nine wickets in the match, but one that was not impossible with Trueman in such outstanding form. The form Trueman showed in 1963 was as consistent as at any other time in his career. This is borne out by the amount of sheer hard work he had to undertake in order to achieve his success. Some bowlers would have wilted under the pressure. Forty and more overs in three out of four Tests is a daunting proportion but Trueman stuck to his task with resolute determination and the results were unqualified success.

From the course of events, it transpired that Trueman had little opportunity to attempt reaching the forty-wicket mark for the series when the final Test was played at the Oval late in August. He was the key man in England's attack and in the tourists' first innings he bowled with his customary verve and tenacity to take 3 for 65 off 26.1 overs. Unfortunately, early on the third morning Trueman twisted his left ankle. The injury was diagnosed as a bruised bone and despite extensive treatment over the weekend there was no sign of a complete recovery. As a result, Trueman could bowl only one over in the West Indies second innings. With England's main attacking force safely out of harm's way, West Indies were able to coast home to a comfortable eight-wicket victory. Their final score of 255 for 2 was an emphatic reminder of the overwhelming superiority of the Caribbean batsmen over the vast majority of England's bowlers and the series was clinched by a decisive three games to one.

The injury at the Oval was a disappointing conclusion to the series for Trueman, but, at the age of thirty-two, he had proved beyond question that he was still the finest fast bowler in England. The critics had never been slow to sharpen their pencils in readiness to malign him and now Trueman was past thirty there was a tendency to write him off as 'past his best' whenever he did not bowl up to his own high standards. Be that as it may, but Trueman had given the perfect answer in 1963 and, what is more, was still breaking records. The three wickets he took in the West Indies first innings at the Oval gave him a total of thirty-four for the series, thus setting a new record number of wickets for a bowler in an England–West Indies rubber. This gave Trueman the unique distinction of holding the wicket-taking records for such series both in England and the West Indies. He had previously set the record for the number of wickets taken on a Caribbean tour, twenty-one, on the 1959–60 trip and to add the home series record to his name as well was a stunning performance for a man reputed to be past his best. Trueman's record in 1963 did not comprise solely of the West Indies series. In 1963 as a whole he took more than sixty Test wickets, a staggering number for a fast bowler and they came from eleven Tests. The eleven were comprised of four against Australia (the First Test was played late in 1962), two against New Zealand and five against West Indies. It was an incredible record of consistency, accuracy and, above all, fitness but the critics tended to forget these marvellous achievements. Just because of Trueman's age they had to assume that he was 'over the hill'. Nothing could have been further from the truth as Trueman's figures very well prove.

In addition to these prizes, Trueman was still the undisputed leader in terms of total Test wickets. His world record total had reached 284 by the end of the 1963 series, far ahead of any other bowler, and he was now within striking distance of the magical, previously undreamed-of, figure of 300 Test wickets. The prime question everybody was asking was simple: when would the triple century arrive? It is absolutely certain that the goal could have been reached far sooner than when it actually did occur because MCC undertook an eight-week, five-Test tour to India early in 1964 under the captaincy of Mike Smith. Trueman, predictably, did not go on the tour, just as he had not gone in 1961–2 to the same continent, and instead the 300th wicket would have to come from one of the Australian touring party due to arrive in England in 1964. Despite the ups and downs of the previous twelve years it was a fitting climax that the most redoubtable opponents of all should present Trueman with the far from easy task of finally reaching the wonderful figure of 300 Test wickets.

AVERAGES FOR 1963 SERIES *v* WEST INDIES: Five Tests, Played Five

Overs	*Mdns*	*Runs*	*Wkts*	*Ave*
236.4	53	594	34	17.47

Inns	*NO*	*Runs*	*HS*	*Ave*
10	1	82	29*	9.11

Catches=3

Match results=England 1, West Indies 3, 1 Match drawn.

Statistics
1 Total Test wickets=284
2 Total catches=60
3 Total runs=933
4 Total appearances=61

N.B.
1 Trueman was the highest English wicket-taker for the eighth time in his career.
2 The total of thirty-four wickets was a new record for the total number of wickets taken in an England–West Indies series and gave Trueman the record at home and in West Indies, a distinction without parallel in the history of Tests between the two countries.

14 Australia, at home, 1964

Trueman had reached the age of thirty-three when the Australian tourists arrived in England for the summer series of 1964 and despite retaining his tremendous fitness, enthusiasm and continued good form with the ball it was clear that Trueman would not continue in the top flight for many more seasons. He was still, by far, the best fast bowler available to the England selectors but young, up-and-coming starlets were knocking at the door, awaiting recognition and the time was not far away when Trueman would have to take his final bow. Already cast aside was Brian Statham who had not played for England since the First Test of 1963 against West Indies and he was not destined to play in any of the Tests against the 1964 Australians. A brilliant, long-standing partnership of great effectiveness was at an end (although Statham did make a belated comeback in the latter half of 1965) and all the evidence pointed to complete reshaping of the England team in the mid-1960s. Trueman only maintained his place in the England team because of his exceptional ability. With a mere sixteen more wickets needed for him to become the first bowler ever to take 300 Test wickets it was imperative that Trueman made the supreme effort in 1964 and it was fitting that the opposition should be the oldest enemy of all, Australia. They would see to it that Trueman did not claim his undeniably well-deserved accolade too easily and it would show that Trueman could keep up his wonderful momentum at an age when the vast majority of fast bowlers are considered to be past their best.

Under the captaincy of Bobby Simpson, the Australians were primarily an experimental party. The retirement of such high-class players as Benaud, Davidson and Harvey had seriously depleted the all-round strength of the side and it was not surprising, when the squad was announced, that eight out of the seventeen players had never previously been to England. When the party was originally released to the media critics instantly slammed it as one of the weakest-ever to represent Australia. While, in terms of matches won, lost or drawn this was partially true, Simpson's men were still more than adequate to fulfil the requirements of the sole object of the exercise, namely to retain the Ashes. They won the series, by virtue of a single victory, and nobody could ask for more.

The question of the worthiness of various touring sides is a vexing one. Comparison achieves little, especially when the respective teams are years apart in having played their individual series and the matter is best left in the singular context of the particular series in which a chosen side has to play. Consequently, as Simpson's team won the 1964, in the wake of much adverse criticism, there could be very little room for complaint afterwards. Simpson and his team accomplished the task that lay before them and it was the perfect answer to all of the pessimists.

The series commenced at Trent Bridge in the first week of June. As a sporting contest the game was ruined by the weather, with some fifteen hours lost in all to the rain, and a result was never likely. Result or not, and despite the restricted amount of playing time, the game did produce some memorable moments, the most remarkable of which instantly became known as the 'Titmus incident'. Although not normally an opener, all-rounder Fred Titmus had hurriedly been deputed to open the innings for England when John Edrich was pronounced unfit to play a little more than an hour before the teams took the field. Dexter won the toss and Titmus filled the opener's role soundly, staying with Boycott for the first hour until he could very easily have been run out. Titmus stayed at the crease and what happened instead was an act of genuine sportsmanship of a type rarely witnessed in international sport.

The incident occurred when Hawke was bowling to Boycott, who played the ball towards Corling at mid-on. Titmus set off for a single and Hawke, in diving for the ball, accidentally knocked him over from behind. Titmus fell in such a way as to prevent Hawke from retrieving the ball and Corling swiftly pounced on the ball to hurl it to wicket-keeper Grout with Titmus still yards out of his ground.

With perfect precision Grout proceeded to make a classic,

graceful wicket-keeper's pass over the top of the stumps without removing the bails. Titmus was allowed to complete the single because of this marvellous piece of sportsmanship and it was an act with which Hawke fully concurred but it was by no means a unanimous Australian decision. Norman O'Neill, fielding in the covers, watched Grout's actions with obvious mixed feeling as his terse comment of 'and I thought this was a bloody Test Match!' amply conveyed. Yet, the incident would not go unnoticed in the England camp. Shades of McGlew, some four years earlier on the very same ground, would have pricked a few consciences, for here was an Australian showing the English the right thing to do!

On a more serious note was Trueman's personal performance in a match destined to be a draw from the start of play on the first day. In the Australian first innings he took 3 for 58, taking his total on to 287, but to the tourists there was evidence that perhaps Trueman's powers were beginning to recede. This was brought to light by Trueman's use of the bouncer which he was still trying to trade as a weapon and did so right up to the last over of the match. O'Neill, one of the finest exponents of the hook shot of his day, received four in succession during Trueman's second over of the second innings. Each one was dispatched to the boundary with electrifying power and by using this form of attack gave a positive appearance to the Australian train of thought.

It may well have been pride rather than good tactics that induced Trueman to persist with such a foolhardy mode of delivery. As the game progressed the pitch had become considerably slower and to continue bowling bouncers on such a deadpan wicket merely provided O'Neill with cannon fodder. At the same time it conveyed the distinct impression to the visitors that the maestro was over the hill. The Australians took heart from what they had seen but with characteristic panache Trueman bounced back in the very next Test to show that he was far from being a spent force and the tourists soon realised the folly of the thoughts. In his own inimitable style, Trueman exploded the theory at the first opportunity, in the Second Test at Lord's. Once more the match was marred by rain, over half of the allotted time being lost and making the result an inevitable draw, but this did not prevent Trueman from making his point in a most positive manner. Play could not begin until the third day, so heavy was the rain, and Dexter immediately put Australia in to bat when he won the toss. The batsmen could master neither the conditions nor, more particularly, Trueman and the innings was completed in less than a day's play with the score reaching a moderate 176 all out.

This was the Trueman of old, using the full range of his skills and talents in complete contrast to his efforts at Nottingham. The blistering pace was not the same as in former years but Trueman used all of his expertise and knowledge in the best possible way. The perfectly balanced run-up and bowling action were still to be seen, although Trueman deliberately shortened the length of his run and, similar with his speed, he cut back on pace and concentrated on cutting the ball off the pitch. By varying his pace and length Trueman was always able to dominate the Australian batsmen and he concluded the innings by bowling Corling to clinch his fifth wicket. The splendid analysis read 25–8–48–5 and the total had crept up to 292, ever-nearer the coveted third century.

England totalled 246 all out in their first innings to take a lead of 70 runs but Australia had little difficulty in clearing the deficit. The second innings total reached 168 for 4 when the rain returned on the last day to signify the end of the game and the second stalemate in succession fizzled out into a tame draw. For Trueman, there was one more wicket in the second innings, giving him a total of 293 wickets to take to Headingley for the Third Test and there was the possibility that he might raise the 300 on his home ground.

Events were to prove the Leeds Test to be the decisive game of the series and for Trueman particularly it was to be a somewhat traumatic experience. Primarily because of the weather, neither side had been able to grasp the initiative in the series but this was to change dramatically in the Third Test. Trueman had bounced back into the limelight at Lord's, and it was ironical that he should receive such a mauling at Headingley that he was summarily dropped, along with Cowdrey, for the Fourth Test. The game was a disaster for Trueman but the fact that Australia won by seven wickets had very little to do with his omission from the side for the next Test. Conversely, it was more by the manner in which Australia gained their victory that caused Trueman's swift dismissal. Australia won by virtue of two principal reasons. First and foremost was a fantastic innings by Peter Burge, which led to the game being tagged as 'Burge's Match', and secondly was the remarkable recovery staged by the last three Australian batsmen in supporting Burge towards the end of the first innings which provided a springboard to eventual success.

Prior to Australia batting, Dexter won the toss and England took first strike to total 268 all out. It was not an immense score by Test Match standards but when the Australian batting collapsed on the second day it began to take on an impressive hue and possibly could have been a winning effort. The slow bowlers had done the damage, notably Titmus who bowled superbly. The net result was that the Australians were tottering at 178 for 7 and it was at this stage of the game that the decisive point arrived. The new ball was due, giving Dexter a double choice in his quest for the last three wickets. He could have left the slow bowlers on, because of the spell Titmus had cast over the batsmen, or he could have brought back Trueman and Flavell to polish off the innings.

There is little doubt as to how the Australians felt about the matter. When Neil Hawke went out to bat at the fall of the seventh wicket there was an atmosphere of complete and utter despair in the tourists' dressing-room. Silence reigned supreme, so low had Australian spirits sunk, and the whole issue appeared to be a lost cause. Contrary to an account of the match written by Australian captain Simpson, Hawke is adamant that he did not receive any instructions whatsoever from Simpson when he went in to bat. The memory of the despondency that pervaded the dressing-room remained etched vividly in his mind, as clear twelve years after the game as the day he went into bat in that Third Test. Hawke could not recall so much as a 'good luck' farewell from his downcast team-mates and the melancholic depression will have affected Simpson as much as anybody. What transpired, therefore, when Hawke joined Burge at the crease was strictly 'off the cuff' but how they made things happen once the pair were together! They proceeded to add 105 runs for the eighth wicket before Hawke was dismissed by Trueman off the last ball of the day and in doing so changed the entire course of the match.

At the beginning of his innings, Hawke played back a number of deliveries from Titmus until, in the eighty-ninth over, Dexter made his monumental decision. Trueman and Flavell were brought back to account for the tail-enders. That was the theory but in practice it was nothing of the sort. To describe simply that both Trueman and Flavell bowled badly would be an understatement close to ridicule for in the following seven overs a staggering 63 runs were added to the score.

At the outset of the partnership Burge had a brief conversation with Hawke. The senior batsman reasoned that there was little to be gained by attempting to shield Hawke from the bowling and told him as much. Hawke was not a novice with the bat, he had a three-figure score to his name in Sheffield Shield cricket, therefore he was well enough equipped in technique to take his chance against the bowling. When the bowling change came, followed by the rapid influx of runs Burge had a second mid-wicket chat with his partner. Short and straight to the point it summed up the situation perfectly, 'I don't know what the hell's happening,' he said, 'but I'm bloody glad!'

The pearls of wisdom uttered by Burge illustrated the Australians' amazement at Dexter's decision. Titmus had the batsmen completely tied down but Trueman and Flavell were allowed to return to the attack and the Australians were off the hook. When the partnership began Burge was 38 not out. At close of play it was 100 not out, the century coming shortly before the end leaving Hawke to play out the remaining deliveries of the day. The stand was worth 105 runs when Hawke faced Trueman for the final ball of the second day.

Normally, the teams would have been off the field for bad light but the batsmen were so much in control, and Burge so near to his century, that they had not appealed against the light. A measure of how dark it actually was can be judged from Hawke being able to distinguish faces in the crowd when people struck a match to light a cigarette. Much nearer than the crowd, Hawke could see Trueman at the end of his run-up. All of the pent-up anger and frustration showed grimly on his face.

Trueman had received a hammering that afternoon and Hawke fully expected a bouncer as Trueman released his strained emotions in a final desperate fling. Instead, he received the perfect outswinger which moved away fractionally from the bat and Parfitt gleefully accepted the chance in the slips. Not all of Trueman's bowling was short-pitched that afternoon, as Hawke readily testified. The last ball of the day was as near perfect as one could ever hope to see.

Burge, meanwhile, was playing the innings of a lifetime. Grout joined him the following morning to add another 89 runs for the ninth wicket and an incredible recovery by Australia was complete with the last three wickets adding 211 runs. Burge was last man out, for 160, and he had seen his side through to a match-winning lead of 121 runs (the game eventually went to Australia by seven wickets) but controversy raged for days as to who was to blame for allowing Australia back into the game. Was it Dexter, for changing the bowling? Was it Trueman and Flavell for bowling so badly? Or, and a point not mooted at the time, was it because of Burge's truly great innings which fully justified his name being appended to the game as a descriptive title?

Inevitably, the man to shoulder the brunt of the blame was Trueman. In similar view to 1961, when Australia had also been in opposition at Old Trafford, he was made the scapegoat. *Wisden* wrote in its match report that Trueman 'fed him (Burge) with a generous supply of long hops' yet no mention is made of Flavell. Nor is it stated that Dexter put himself on to bowl when the move was seen not to work. Trueman cannot be whitewashed from the affair and neither can Flavell be wholly blamed but a study of the views of two of the players who took part in the match will give a clearer, more reasoned opinion on the outcome of the match.

The Australian point of view has already been seen from Neil Hawke's account of his ninth wicket partnership with Burge. From the England side Peter Parfitt reached a number of definite conclusions about the game. In the first instance, he thought Dexter's decision to bring back the pacemen was the right one under the circumstances prevailing. When the move did not meet with success the two bowlers switched ends, again without reward. Dexter then went on to bowl himself but by that time Burge was in sparkling form. Parfitt acknowledges Burge's innings as being brilliant. It was a match-winning effort and that, rather than rank bad bowling was the main reason for Australia's success.

Apart from the players' views, the one person who had the final word on the pitch is Dexter by virtue of his position as captain. In any game, the man who shoulders the ultimate responsibility must be the captain. If any blame is to be apportioned it must go to the man who manipulates the players, not the players who are manipulated. That is not to say that Dexter should have been dropped, he was a fine player and first-rate captain. The results are past history and the consequences were that two stalwarts of the England side for years gone by, Trueman and Cowdrey, were dropped for the Fourth Test but it was a bitter pill for Trueman to swallow. The final irony was that his total of Test wickets had reached 297 after the Leeds' Test and to be so close to the 300 and then be dropped when within one match of reaching the goal was harsh justice to a tireless servant of English cricket.

Being dropped was a blessing in disguise for Trueman, notwithstanding the record being so near at hand. The Fourth Test was played at Old Trafford and the Australians, with their one-nil lead in the series, set out from the start to avoid defeat. They batted well into the third day amassing 656 for 8 declared with Simpson scoring a remorseless 311 and a draw was always going to be the end result. Peter Parfitt summed up the match admirably by describing it as 'the most boring Test Match I ever played in', and that is condemnation enough of Australian tactics.

Trueman and Cowdrey were recalled for the Fifth Test at the Oval in a last-ditch attempt to salvage the series and immediately Trueman had the nation guessing. Would he, at last, reach the 300th mark? Millions saw him do so but the events leading up to the occasion had all the markings of a Shakespearian tragedy. There was comedy, drama, near despair, then ecstasy as Trueman finally reached the Everest of his career.

Events began to roll several days before the final Test began when the Australians were playing Yorkshire at Bradford.

Trueman was not playing for his county but during the game he joined the visitors in their dressing-room. The topic of conversation was naturally centred around the 300 figure still to be attained and although the team for the Oval Test had still to be announced Trueman already knew he would be picked. It would be all or nothing in that Test and one of the Australians joining in the banter was Neil Hawke. Casually, he said to Trueman, 'Well, if you only want one when I go in I'll make sure you get it'. Many a true word is spoken in jest and Hawke could have had no idea just how true his words would be. Prophets are few and far between but there was one present from Adelaide sitting in a Bradford dressing-room in August 1964.

The real drama began to unfold on the third day of the Fifth Test. Prior to this Hawke had already been in the limelight, taking 6 for 47, as England were bowled out 182. Australia cleared the total for the loss of three wickets and as lunchtime approached on the third day they were well in command. Dexter was in a quandary as to who he should ask to bowl. The new ball was not due for three overs and he decided to ask Parfitt to bowl his off-breaks but Trueman, who was standing close by heard this and immediately said, 'I don't mind bowling.' Bowl he did and with what results!

Previously, Trueman had been ineffective; now he was revitalised. He roared to the wicket and Redpath's middle stump was flattened. That was number 298. Graham McKenzie walked to the wicket, took guard and Trueman sped to the wicket again. He bowled, McKenzie snicked and Cowdrey took the catch as easily as he might have plucked an apple from a tree. How the crowd roared. Number 299 and the 300 could come with a hat-trick. It was a breathtaking prospect but even more amazing was the name of the next batsman to go in—Neil Hawke!

Fortunately or unfortunately, whichever the case may be, the umpires decided there was not enough time for Hawke to reach the crease and lunch was taken. Trueman had to sweat through the most nerve-racking forty minutes of his life and it was no less a test of nerves for the big Australian waiting to go in to bat. The interlude did nothing for his appetite because Hawke simply could not face the prospect of eating. He was only too well aware that when the players went back on to the field after the luncheon interval the eyes of the world would be focused on him and Trueman alone.

There was no question of Trueman being 'given' anything. What had been said a week earlier was no more than a jovial remark, a passing comment but fate had showed its hand to play a strange trick on Neil Hawke. Unlike all good fairy-tales the hat-trick did not materialise. The first ball after lunch sailed harmlessly past the off-stump, and countless thousands up and down Britain settled down to await the great moment. It was the sixth and final time that a Test Match hat-trick had been 'on' for Trueman, but as always, the goal eluded him. Not the 300th wicket, however. A short while later Hawke edged a ball from Trueman into the ever-safe hands of Cowdrey at first slip and there it was.

N. J. N. Hawke   c Cowdrey   b Trueman   14

Number 300, for all the world to see and how fitting that another England veteran, the recalled Colin Cowdrey, should assist Trueman to accomplish the feat. Trueman had achieved what many thought was impossible and his name would be immortal in cricket history because of it.

What of Hawke's reaction? He was the first to shake Trueman by the hand, say, 'Well done, mate,' then quietly leave the stage. As Hawke remarked afterwards, by becoming Trueman's 300th wicket he was allotted his own special place in cricket history. More than anything else Neil Hawke did in his Test career, he would always be remembered as the man Trueman dismissed to gain his 300th Test wicket. Hawke's own comment on the achievement was honest and direct, 'As one who took less than one hundred Test wickets I know what he must have put into it,' a fine compliment from a man who was good enough to play for Australia twenty-seven times and take ninety-one Test wickets.

The real glory on that day could belong only to one man, Fred Trueman. He could hold his arms aloft, pointing to the heavens, and bask in the glory of the crowd's applause. It had taken Trueman thirteen years of back-breaking toil to achieve what no other man had accomplished before him and his name would always be synonymous with the giants of the fast bowling fraternity. After the match there was a touching finale from Trueman when he sent Neil Hawke a bottle of champagne which Hawke still has to this day, unopened, at his home in Adelaide.

As for the match, it was a disappointment for England. Rain washed out play on the final day, after Trueman had completed the Australian first innings by having Corling caught by Parfitt and England had reached 381 for 4 in their second innings. Australia had won the series by one game to nil and kept the Ashes they already held but in Trueman's case the season would hold far sweeter memories than the disappointment of not winning back the Ashes.

When the curtain came down on the 1964 season, one of the finest fast bowlers ever to grace a cricket field had reached the summit of his career. The third 100 wickets had covered the period stretching from 21 June 1962 to 15 August 1964, encompassing only eighteen Test Matches. This was four games fewer than his second 100 had taken and an astonishing seven fewer than the first 100. Thus, the average number of wickets per Test had risen from 4.00 to 5.5. For a man in the obvious twilight of his international career it was almost unbelievable that Trueman should be taking wickets at a greater rate than at any other stage of his career but the bare facts show it to be true. At an age when the majority of fast bowlers would be pensioned off Trueman was still striving at his work and taking wickets by the handful. With no false justification could it be said that the world had never before seen anything quite like F. S. Trueman; he was a man alone among the great names of fast bowling.

AVERAGES FOR 1964 SERIES *v* AUSTRALIA: Five Tests, Played Four

Overs	*Mdns*	*Runs*	*Wkts*	*Ave*
133.3	25	399	17	23.47

Inns	*NO*	*Runs*	*HS*	*Ave*
6	1	42	14	8.40

Catches=3

Match results=England 0, Australia 1, 4 Matches drawn.

Statistics
1 Total Test wickets=301
2 Total catches=63
3 Total runs=975
4 Total appearances=65

N.B. Trueman was the leading English wicket-taker in a series for the ninth and last time in his career.

15 New Zealand, at home, 1965

MCC had arranged a winter tour to South Africa following the 1964 Australian series, embracing a full programme including five Tests. In the four short weeks between the home season ending and the touring party being announced Trueman could revel in the glory of his unique wicket-taking exploits but the euphoria was to last but a very short time. Trueman's name, as so often before, was not on the list.

His omission from successive touring parties had become almost standard practice, with the exception of the most important trips to Australia and the Caribbean, and in keeping with the tradition the reasons bandied about for Trueman not going to the Republic were nothing more than the flimsiest of excuses which bear no substantial weight under close scrutiny. Trueman did not have the automatic right to be chosen for the 1964–5 tour to South Africa. No person should ever be accorded such status, irrespective of his past achievements, and it has often been quoted that sentiment has no place in sport, although a very close parallel to this occurred when Alec Bedser was taken to Australia in 1954–5 after turning down a tour to the West Indies the previous winter. However, despite the critics saying that Trueman was too old at the age of thirty-three in 1964 to undertake the tour he had one all-important factor in his favour—he was still the best bowler at England's disposal.

Statistics can often be interpreted in a misleading manner but the bowling averages for 1964 and 1965 for three individual players cannot be seen in any other light except to show Trueman as the undisputed leader of the pack. In 1964 Trueman's total number of first class wickets was 121, which was practically double the number reached by two of the fast bowlers originally chosen for the tour, J. S. E. Price and A. G. Nicholson. At the time age was the predominate reason given for Trueman's absence from the party but this myth was exploded when, after Nicholson was forced to withdraw from the tour because of a back injury, N. I. Thomson, of Sussex, who was then thirty-five years old and totally devoid of Test Match experience either at home or abroad was chosen as replacement!

Thomson was a very consistent performer in county cricket. He took over 100 wickets in a season on twelve consecutive occasions but there could be no logical explanation for taking a 35-year-old pace bowler on a five-Test tour who had yet to make his international debut. One possibility is that Thomson was receiving a bonus from the selectors at the end of a fine county career while Trueman was left at home to reflect on the glories of his past exploits in sixty-five Tests. In the opinion of Peter Parfitt, who went on the tour, the decision not to take Trueman was beyond comprehension and when an England player of his experience takes such a view there has to be something radically wrong with MCC's selection procedures.

Parfitt readily acknowledges that Nicholson, Price and Thomson were all very good bowlers in their own right but when it comes to a question of comparison with Trueman it is a vastly different story. By no stretch of the imagination could any of them, at any stage of their careers, be classed as equal to Trueman. Furthermore, and much more important in Parfitt's opinion, could any of them expect to be anywhere near as effective as Trueman when playing abroad? Their lack of experience alone would bear out that point. Of the three selected players, only Price had played Test cricket previously: four times in India in 1963–4 and twice against Australia in 1964 and he alone could justify selection as an up-and-coming young fast bowler. With Nicholson and Thomson brand new to Test cricket, Parfitt's view that 'there was no way any English bowler could be better abroad than Trueman' is the crux of the matter.

Another factor apparently ignored by the selectors was Trueman's performances over the 1964 season when compared to the other bowlers picked for the tour. Any amount of conjecture will not solve the riddle of Trueman's omission from the party but one indisputable fact remains: he was by far the most successful bowler of the quartet under scrutiny not only in 1964, on which figures the selections could have been based, but also the following year. The following figures show why:

EXTRACT FROM FIRST-CLASS BOWLING AVERAGES 1964

	Overs	*Mdns*	*Runs*	*Wkts*	*Ave*
A. G. Nicholson	503.4	145	976	70	13.94
N. I. Thomson	857.5	281	1,740	109	15.96
F. S. Trueman	556.2	122	1,344	104	17.28
J. S. E. Price	647	137	1,566	60	26.10

Also Trueman played in four Tests and Price in two Tests against Australia to gain the following averages:

	Overs	*Mdns*	*Runs*	*Wkts*	*Ave*
F. S. Trueman	133.3	25	399	17	23.47
J. S. E. Price	66	6	250	4	62.50

Thus, Trueman took marginally more wickets in total than Thomson in 1964 and a great many more than either Nicholson or Price. History shows that Thomson went to South Africa but in the light of the considered comments made by alleged experts that Trueman was 'past it' in 1964 it is worth noting also the averages for the following season, the summer after the South African tour:

EXTRACT FROM FIRST-CLASS BOWLING AVERAGES 1965

	Overs	*Mdns*	*Runs*	*Wkts*	*Ave*
F. S. Trueman	568	140	1,307	115	11.36
N. I. Thompson	719.5	197	1,535	72	21.35
J. S. E. Price	303.4	69	781	33	23.68

Also Trueman played in two Tests against New Zealand to gain the following averages:

	Overs	*Mdns*	*Runs*	*Wkts*	*Ave*
F. S. Trueman	96.3	23	237	6	39.50

Trueman's total number of wickets in 1965 was exactly the same as in 1964, a season in which only Thomson could approach near to him while in 1965 the Sussex man was nearly fifty wickets adrift. Ironically, it was Trueman who was alleged to be the spent force but he still came out well on top, indisputably England's foremost bowler and at the end of the numbers game there remains but one question. What possible justification could the selectors have for first choosing Nicholson and then replacing him with Thomson instead of taking Trueman to South Africa?

It was not quite the end of the road for Trueman, for all that he missed the 1964 tour. In 1965 a relatively new arrangement was adopted by MCC in having two Test teams visiting England in the same summer. It was the first time this had occurred since 1912 when a triangular tournament was held between England, Australia and South Africa. The venture was considered a failure and it was not until 1965 that the idea was resurrected and then not on a tournament basis. New Zealand and South Africa were the visitors and each side took one half of the season during which they played their own three-match series against England. It proved to be a much better format than the one used in the distant past and Trueman took part in the first two Tests of the summer, against New Zealand. They were his swansong in Test cricket. The second Test at Lord's was his sixty-seventh and last appearance for England and the only consolation for Trueman was that he was on the winning side. In every other way it was a disappointing end to an illustrious career.

England won both of the Tests in which Trueman played, the first at Edgbaston by nine wickets and the second at Lord's by seven wickets but for a man of Trueman's stature the games were a sad finale to a career which was unrivalled in the history of cricket. At Edgbaston he had figures of 1 for 49 and 3 for 79 while at Lord's they were even more disappointing. Out of a meagre first innings total of 175 all out by New Zealand in the Second Test, Trueman had figures of 19.5–8–40–2. They were his last wickets in Test cricket. In the New Zealanders' second innings Trueman toiled away for twenty-six overs without claiming a single wicket. His last analysis, 26–4–69–0, settled the matter once and for all for the selectors and he was never picked for England again.

On initial inspection, it would appear to be a meek, even miserable, departure from the Test Match arena by Trueman but Peter Parfitt supplied the perfect appreciation of the situation when this book was in the embryo stage, 'It is not the last match that counts,' he said, 'but all that had gone before. That is what Trueman will be remembered for most of all.' How very true. Devoid of wickets in his last spell of bowling for England did not make for a fairy-tale ending to Trueman's career but cricket history would show much more than that final game.

There was one satisfactory point to be gleaned by Trueman from the last appearance in that he managed to keep intact a record which stretched all the way back to his very first Test for England in 1952. The two wickets that Trueman claimed in the New Zealand first innings on his last appearance for England meant that he had never failed to take a wicket in any of the sixty-seven Tests in which he played.

From 5 June 1952 until 22 June 1965 was the full extent of Trueman's career, giving him fourteen years of cricket at the highest possible level but how much he gave back to the game is incalculable. From P. Umrigar c Evans b Trueman 8 to R. O. Collinge b Trueman 7, first wicket to last, covered the sum total of Trueman's 307 Test wickets, a feat without parallel up to the time of his retirement and a record still to be bettered by a fast bowler. Whether Trueman claimed five wickets or none in his last appearance for England it mattered little. Enough had been accomplished by Trueman over the years for his name to be revered long after Richard Collinge had his stumps spreadeagled at Lord's in 1965 when Trueman took his last Test wicket. The trials and tribulations, humiliations and rebuffs, idolisation and glory were at an end and the world of cricket had seen the last of one of the finest, most exciting, and flamboyant fast bowlers ever to tread the turf of a Test Match cricket ground.

AVERAGES FOR 1965 SERIES *v* NEW ZEALAND: Three Tests, Played Two

Overs	*Mdns*	*Runs*	*Wkts*	*Ave*
96.3	23	237	6	39.50

Inns	*NO*	*Runs*	*HS*	*Ave*
2	0	6	3	3.00

Catches=1

Match results=England 3, New Zealand 0.

Statistics
1 Total Test wickets=307
2 Total catches= 64
3 Total runs= 981
4 Total appearances=67

The long run-up was over, run for the last time in a Test Match and completed in terms of years spent as a number of the England team but what remains at the end of it? The answer is another question; just how good was F. S. Trueman? In comparison to other fast bowlers Trueman must of necessity rank among the giants of all time; his record alone justifies the claim but for substantiation Trueman's overall career must be assessed from two widely differing points before this falls into place. The first is by viewing the opposition he played against and the second is by way of a testimonial from a fellow professional.

Trueman played Test cricket against every Test-playing country in the world and over the years spanned by his career Australia and West Indies were the dominant teams in addition to England. India, Pakistan and New Zealand were very weak while South Africa were only marginally stronger. Consequently, Trueman would normally be expected to claim the majority of his wickets against these teams rather than the two stronger countries. This was not the case, due to a number of circumstances which appear tantamount to Trueman having been deliberately kept away from the weaker sides, especially when England were playing abroad. Trueman was never chosen to tour India, Pakistan or South Africa with the result that his total appearances against each of those teams do not reach double figures. His appearances were limited to four against Pakistan, six against South Africa and nine against India although throughout Trueman's career England played a total of fifty-one Tests against these countries. The situation is best documented by means of a chart.

RECORD OF ALL TESTS PLAYED BY ENGLAND *v* INDIA, PAKISTAN AND SOUTH AFRICA 1952–65

Opponents	*Number of Tests*	*Venue*	*Trueman's appearances*	*Number outstanding*
India	19	9 At home 10 Abroad	9 At home 0 Abroad	10
Pakistan	12	9 At home 3 Abroad	4 At home 0 Abroad	8
South Africa	20	10 At home 10 Abroad	6 At home 0 Abroad	14
Totals	51	28 At home 23 Abroad	19 At home 0 Abroad	32

N.B. These figures do not include the 1965 home series against South Africa because Trueman had made his last appearance before that series began.

The crux of the matter lies in the word 'abroad'. Twenty-three possible appearances disappeared instantly because Trueman's presence was not wanted in various touring parties. This was a recurring feature throughout Trueman's career and it not only denied half of the cricketing countries of the world from seeing him play Test cricket but it also took valuable opportunities away from Trueman of adding to his rich harvest of wickets.

Five overseas trips were missed in all to the above listed countries alone and when they, and the numbers of Tests played, are added to the remaining two tours missed it will be seen that Trueman's inclusion in an MCC touring party was only made when the strength of the opposition demanded nothing short of the best. Because of this Trueman was robbed of some twenty to twenty-five extra appearances which would have taken him well towards the century mark instead of the sixty-seven he actually made. Again, a chart gives the clearest summary:

RECORD OF ALL OFFICIAL MCC TEST TOURS 1952–65

Venue	*Year*	*Number of Tests*	*Trueman's appearances*	*Number outstanding*
West Indies	1953–4	5	3	2
	1959–60	5	5	0
Australia	1954–5	5	0	5
	1958–9	5	3	2
	1962–3	5	5	0
New Zealand	1954–5	2	0	2
	1958–9	2	2	0
	1962–3	3	2	1
South Africa	1956–7	5	0	5
	1964–5	5	0	5
India	1961–2	5	0	5
	1963–4	5	0	5
Pakistan	1961–2	3	0	3
Totals		55	20	35

If including the New Zealand tours, which invariably come at the end of an Australian tour, Trueman made six overseas trips in all, approximately half of the thirteen possible. Whereas the first chart encompasses Tests played at home and abroad against three of the 'weaker' countries at that time, the second chart is solely concerned with Tests played abroad against every

Test-playing country. Significantly the number of Tests which Trueman missed is practically identical in both cases.

The picture emerging is two-fold. In the first instance Trueman was not given the opportunity to play abroad as much as could have been possible, and secondly that the greater proportion of his Test appearances were made in England. The home series played during Trueman's career covered a total of sixty-six Tests, of which he played in forty-seven and again there is a high average of omissions in those totals. Not all of the omissions were justified but, by the same token, Trueman could not have expected to be picked for every one of England's 121 Tests played throughout his career. However, by using the above figures it is fair to say that Trueman was definitely deprived of a total approaching approximately forty more appearances than he actually made. He actually missed a total of fifty-two, therefore forty could be construed as a conservative estimate and when that happens to England's premier bowler there is something radically wrong. On averages alone with those extra appearances Trueman would have taken his final total of Test wickets to around the 500 mark! And people thought 300 would be impossible to reach.

The one consolation to be gained from this catalogue of omissions is that it can never be said that Trueman picked up his wickets against the weaker countries. His combined number of wickets against India, Pakistan and New Zealand brought him less than one-third of his 307 Test wickets while the much stronger opposition of Australia and West Indies provided over half—165, in fact. That alone proves his worth as a fast bowler and nothing can detract from it.

On the question of comparison with other fast bowlers the answer does not come easily. In his era, Trueman was unquestionably without peer and it is on that basis that he is best judged. To go back to the turn of the century would be quite meaningless. Conditions were vastly different, the game was played in a completely different style and most important of all is the fact that Test Match opposition was then greatly less in numbers than at the time of Trueman's career. Only England, Australia and South Africa were playing Test cricket and because of this the standards and records set were of a varying nature. West Indies did not begin touring England until 1928, India until 1932 and Pakistan until 1952 and only with the full range of opposition to play against could the greats of yesteryear expect an exact comparison with Trueman since they played a mere handful of teams.

With this in mind, comparisons, therefore, have to be made with bowlers near or actually from Trueman's own era for them to have any bearing on the matter. The outstanding fast bowlers since the war have come from three countries (other than England) namely, Australia, West Indies and South Africa. From down under come Lindwall, Miller and Davidson; the Caribbean islands have produced Hall and Griffith, while the best from South Africa was Neil Adcock.

To begin with the most explosive bowler first, the choice must be Wes Hall. He was a superb athlete, one of the finest to play Test cricket and with his tremendous speed was probably faster than Trueman. Hall had a beautiful, very fast run-up and two contemporary Test cricketers, Neil Hawke and Peter Parfitt, share the opinion that he was one of the fastest men in the world on his day. However, speed was his prime asset. Hawke says, 'You could tell from his run-up alone when Hall was going to slip a really fast one in.' Speed is a considerable weapon, but alone it does not make the all-round bowler. Trueman, on the other hand, had a brilliant control over his pace. Fast off-breaks, cutters and slower balls would be used in between his fastest deliveries which would cause batsmen manifold problems. Hall's record for the West Indies was good but it could not match Trueman's in quantity or consistency and, fine bowler though he was, he had to take second place to his Yorkshire counterpart.

Hall's chief comrade-in-arms was Charlie Griffith, who was also tremendously fast. However, the means by which he achieved his speed were somewhat suspect and there appears to be little doubt that he threw the ball, thus making any comparison with Trueman meaningless. Both Parfitt and Hawke played against Griffith. Their opinions are enlightening with Parfitt saying, 'Griffith was the most lethal projector of a cricket ball I have ever seen.' Moving on to Hawke, he puts the question beyond all doubt.

When playing against West Indies in a Test series the Australian team undertook a simple experiment. The results prove conclusively that Griffith threw and Hawke related the following account to show how easy it was to prove the case. The players first acquired a photograph of a javelin thrower at the instant of projecting the javelin into flight. Then they took a photograph of Griffith in his delivery stride about to release the cricket ball and superimposed one photograph on top of the other. Amazingly, Griffith's arm was in exactly the same position as that of the javelin thrower. Says Hawke of this, quite correctly, 'The ultimate proof comes when one asks the question, "Has anybody suggested that an athlete ever bowled a javelin?" '.

To be perfectly fair to both Hawke and Griffith it must be stated that this view has been held by Hawke for a considerable time and is supported by a welter of photographic evidence. In his own words he sums up the situation as follows. 'This is not an attempt to stab Charlie in the back because he is a good friend of mine but is an opinion backed up by evidence both visual and photographic which I've always felt free to express.'

Moving on to the Australian trio of Lindwall, Miller and Davidson, three outstanding cricketers come under scrutiny. Davidson was not quite as fast as the former pair but Parfitt rated him as the most dangerous new ball bowler in the world, playing when he did from 1953–62. In addition all three were more than useful when batting and this gives them an edge over Trueman, who although he often scored valuable runs for England, never managed to reach a Test half-century in his career. Miller scored nearly 3,000 runs and Lindwall 1,500 runs in Test cricket, considerably more than Trueman, but as it is the bowling which is the prime feature Trueman retains his lead. Lindwall concluded his career with 228 wickets, Davidson 186, and Miller 170 all of which trail well behind Trueman's final count.

The final contemporary of Trueman's is Neil Adcock from South Africa. He was the Republic's finest post-war fast bowler until Peter Pollock appeared on the scene shortly before South Africa ceased playing Test cricket. Adcock bowled with fair pace and in 1960 took more wickets in a series against England than Trueman could muster. Adcock was good, but from his total of twenty-six Tests could never expect to reap the rewards that Trueman enjoyed. Partially, the blame for this lay with South Africa because that country would only play against 'white' teams and if the colour of a man's skin defines how good a cricketer he is it is perhaps better that South Africa no longer figures in world sport. Until there is a change of policy from their leaders, South African sportsmen of the calibre of people like Adcock will never have the chance to compete against the best in the world, which is exactly what happened when the South African fast bowler was playing his Test cricket. From his performance on record, it is still doubtful if Adcock could ever be classed as an equal to Trueman but there can be no doubt that he possessed a lot of ability.

No, Trueman remains on a pinnacle all alone. Even since his retirement very few quick bowlers have appeared to challenge his supremacy. Lillee possibly may have done so but fitness was not his strong point. The speed was there and a perfect bowling action but his rather slim physique (for a fast bowler) could not withstand the rigours of full-time Test cricket. From the Caribbean have come bowlers of the calibre of Roberts, Holding and Daniel. Time is on their side to make an impact on the game but it is time that will have the final word, for it will take a good many years of playing Test cricket before anyone will be able to say, 'I've beaten Trueman's record.' In fact, it is doubtful if a fast bowler to match Trueman's record will be seen for many, many years, if it ever comes to pass at all.

In the opening chapter the word 'great' was purposely omitted from all allusions to Fred Trueman. Now it must be used. The final word goes to Peter Parfitt, whose comments and opinions have frequently been in evidence in this book. He played both in the same England team and against Trueman at county level on numerous occasions and is in a perfect position to judge the qualities of Trueman's bowling. Parfitt played against every Test-playing country in an official Test during his thirty-seven Test career with England and this quote is testimony to the talents of one Frederick Sewards Trueman. 'I have no hesitation in saying that during the sixteen years I played cricket he was the greatest fast bowler I have ever seen.'

Index

Adcock, N.A.T., 127, 216, 217
Adelaide, 56, 73, 177, 180, 203, 205
Alabaster, J.C., 182
Alexander, G., 110, 118, 120-1
Alim-ud-Din, 164-5
Allen, D.A., 110-11, 117, 121, 147-148, 155-6, 160, 163-5, 175, 184-6
Apte, A.L., 91
Archer, R.G., 27
Auckland, 81, 180
Australia, 13, 15, 19, 22, 24-8, 31, 41-9, 64, 68-9, 71-80, 83, 95, 97-108, 122, 124, 134, 138, 141-59, 201-18
Averages, for each Series:
  v.Australia, 28-31, 49, 79, 156-7, 179, 205-6
  v. India, 23-106
  v. New Zealand, 69, 83, 182, 212
  v. Pakistan, 167
  v. South Africa, 44, 138-9
  v. West Indies, 40, 60, 123, 194

Baig, A.A., 85, 91, 93-4
Bailey, T.E., 26, 31-3, 35-6, 45-6, 54-5, 62, 65, 77, 82
Barnes, S.F., 138
Barrington, K.F., 86, 88, 90, 93, 110, 112, 120, 143, 156, 170, 176
Bedser, A.V., 15, 25-6, 137-8, 162, 167, 177, 207
Benaud, R., 72, 76, 78, 140-44, 147-149, 151, 155-6, 169, 177, 195
Bombay, 173
Booth, B.C., 141, 175
Borde, C.G., 86-7, 90-1, 93
Boycott, G., 196
Bradman, Sir D.G., 53, 70
Bridgetown, 33, 110
Brisbane, 15, 71, 169, 173, 178, 183, 186
Buller, J.S., 129-30
Burge, P.J., 46, 141, 146, 170, 199-202
Burke, J.W., 46, 73-5, 77-8
Butcher, B.F., 189

Carew, M.C., 184, 189
Charran Singh, 113
Christchurch, 80-1, 160, 180-1
Close, D.B., 91
Coldwell, L., 163, 175-7
Collinge, R.O., 211
Compton, D.C.S., 26-7, 31
Contractor, N.J., 93, 95
Corling, G.E., 196, 198, 205
Cowdrey, M.C., 52-4, 63, 72-3, 75, 77-8, 86, 89, 90, 92-3, 96, 109, 110, 115-16, 118, 120-2, 131, 134-137, 141-2, 144, 147-9, 151, 158, 160, 164, 174-5, 180, 186, 198, 202-4

Daniel, W.W., 218
D'Arcy, J.W., 65, 68
Davidson, A.K., 27, 78, 144-5, 147, 149, 151, 155-6, 169-70, 177, 195, 216-17
Dexter, E.R., 72, 80, 82, 92, 94, 110, 112, 120, 127, 143-4, 152, 156, 160-1, 163, 165-6, 169, 176, 180, 185, 189, 196, 198-203
Dunedin, 80

Edgbaston, 52, 62, 64, 127, 131, 141, 144-5, 156, 188-9, 210
Edrich, J.H., 196
Edrich, W.J., 26
Elliot, C., 133
Evans, T.G., 14, 18, 26, 31-2, 46, 52, 74, 82, 86

Favell, L.E., 72
Flavell, J.A., 152, 199-201
Frindall, W., 155

Gaekwad, D.K., 84, 87, 89-90, 95
Georgetown, 33-4, 112, 113, 118
Ghorpade, J.M., 91, 96
Gibbs, L.R., 9, 10, 183, 185, 189
Gilchrist, R., 57
Goddard, J.D., 50, 56-7, 183
Goddard, T.L., 130, 136
Gover, A.R., 126

Grace, W.G., 7
Graveney, T.W., 26, 31, 55-6, 58, 71, 74-5, 78, 160, 163, 165, 173
Greenhough, T., 86-8, 96
Griffin, G.M., 83, 125-7, 129-31, 140
Griffith, C.C., 183, 185, 216-7
Grout, A.W.T., 142, 145, 147, 149, 196-7, 201
Gupte, S.P., 94

Hall, W.W., 108, 109, 110, 111, 121, 178, 183, 186, 216
Halley's Comet, 7-8
Hanif Mohammad, 160, 164, 166
Harris, R.M., 81
Harvey, R.N., 46, 77, 141-2, 144-9, 169, 195
Hassett, A.L., 27
Hawke, N.J.N., 9, 178, 196, 199-201, 203-5, 216-17
Hazare, V.S., 15-16
Headingley, 14-15, 17, 20, 46, 56, 58, 65, 89, 91, 146, 151, 157, 164, 191, 198, 202
Hobbs, Sir J.B. 137
Holding, M.A., 218
Hole, G.B., 27
Horton, M.J., 86, 88
Hough, K.W., 80-2
Hunte, C.C., 104, 117, 120-1, 184, 187, 189
Hutton, Sir L., 25-8, 31, 35, 37-9, 56, 82, 89, 92, 137

Illingworth, R., 62, 92, 96, 103, 143, 175, 177
Imtiaz Ahmed, 160
India, 10, 13-22, 24, 38-9, 67, 82-96, 105-13, 135, 137-8, 146, 158

Jackson, H.L., 147-9
Javed Burki, 159, 161, 163-5
Johannesburg, 137
Jones, E., 125

Kanhai, R.B., 109, 114, 117-18, 184, 189
Karachi, 166
King, F.M., 34
King, L.A., 183
Kirpal Singh, A.G., 88

Laker, J.C., 27, 31-2, 46, 49, 58, 62, 64-6, 68, 71-3, 77, 82, 136, 138, 185
Larwood, H., 17, 19, 20
Lawry, W.M., 137, 141, 145, 147-148, 170, 176
Lee, F., 129-30
Lillee, D.K., 218
Lindwall, R.R., 13, 25, 45, 74, 178, 216-17
Loader, P.J., 57, 62, 76, 82, 130
Lock, G.A.R., 26-7, 31, 46, 58, 62, 64-8, 71-4, 80-1, 125, 146-8, 191
Lords, 7, 16-17, 43-6, 49, 54, 64, 66, 85, 87, 94, 125, 126, 129, 144, 146, 161-2, 185, 197-8, 210-11

McDonald, C.C., 49, 74-5, 77-8, 145, 147-8
McGlew, D.J., 125, 127-8, 130, 132-134, 136, 197
McInnes, M., 74-5, 82
MacKay, K.D. 72-3, 142, 149
McKenzie, G.D., 147, 155, 170, 203
McLean, R.A., 132, 135
McMorris, E.D., 110, 120, 184
McWatt, C.A., 113
Meckiff, I., 83
Melbourne, 76, 115, 125, 137, 173-4
Miller, K.R., 13, 46, 178, 216-17
Miller, L.S., 63-5
Milton, C.A., 82, 86
Moir, A.M., 68
Morris, A.R., 27
Mortimore, J.B., 76, 91, 94
Moss, A.E., 31-3, 45, 86, 88, 90-1, 110, 121-2, 127, 131, 133
Moyes, A.G., 15
Murray, J.T., 143, 164, 176
Mushtaq Mohammad, 160, 166

Nadkarni, B.P., 86-7, 90, 93, 96
Nasim-Ul-Ghani, 163, 166
New Zealand, 41-2, 59, 61-70, 76, 78-83, 85, 95, 105, 135, 137-8, 178-9, 210-18
Nicholson, A.G., 207-10
Norfolk, Duke of, 168-70

Old Trafford, 7, 18, 66, 91, 94, 135, 137, 151, 184-5, 202
O'Linn, S., 132-4
O'Neill, N.C., 72, 77, 146-9, 170, 174, 197
Otago, 79
Oval, The, 7, 21, 24-5, 28, 53, 58, 95, 135, 137, 151, 167, 192-3, 203

Pairaudeau, B.H., 57
Pakistan, 41-2, 113, 158-67
Palmer, C.H., 37
Parfitt, P.H., 9, 159-60, 164-5, 173, 176, 182, 201-5, 208, 211, 216-18
Parks, J.M., 121-2, 127
Petrie, E.C., 80-1
Playle, W.R., 66
Ponsford, W.H., 53
Port-of-Spain, (Trinidad), 33, 34, 36, 38, 108, 112, 113-14, 119, 122
Pothecary, J.E., 137
Price, J.S.E., 207-9
Pullar, G., 89-90, 92, 96, 111, 116, 120-1, 136-7, 143, 145, 148, 151, 156, 165, 170

Ramadhin, S., 52-3, 57
Redpath, I.R., 203
Reid, J.R., 61, 64-5, 68, 81
Rhodes, H.J., 89-90, 92-4
Rhodes, W., 137
Richardson, P.E., 58, 75
Roberts, A.M.E., 218
Robins, R.W.V., 107
Rorke, G.F., 78
Roy, P., 53, 84, 86-8, 91, 137

Sabina Park, (Jamaica), 32, 35-6, 39, 114, 118
Saeed Ahmed, 164-5
Scorecards: England v.
a India, 19
b S. Africa, 132-3
c Australia, 150
d Pakistan, 162
e N. Zealand, 181
f W. Indies, 187-8, 190
Shackleton, D., 187, 189
Shadid, M., 166
Shepherd, B.K., 177
Sheppard, Rev D.S., 165, 170, 175
Simpson, R.B., 137, 141-2, 147, 149, 152, 174, 195-6, 199, 202
Smith, D.V., 56
Smith, M.J.K., 92, 96, 112, 121, 122, 129-30, 193
Smith, O.G., 52, 56-7
Sobers, G.S., 103, 114-15, 117, 184-5, 189
Soloman, J.S., 112
South Africa, 41-4, 49, 64, 68, 82, 95, 108, 123-40, 197, 217
Sparling, J.J., 66
Spooner, R.T., 31
Statham, J.B, 31-2, 34-5, 43-5, 54, 56, 62, 67, 72-6, 82, 86-8, 95, 96, 108, 110, 112, 113, 115, 117, 119, 122, 126-7, 129, 131-3, 135-8, 142, 144-6, 152, 156, 158, 160, 164-5, 167, 175, 177-80, 185, 195
Subba Row, R., 82, 96, 109, 142, 143, 151, 156
Surendranath, R., 94-5
Sutcliffe, B., 61, 66, 81
Suttle, K., 31
Swanton, E.W., 39
Swetman, R., 72, 77, 94, 96
Sydney, 70-1, 79, 115, 175, 177-8

Tamhane, N.S., 90, 95
Tayfield, H.J., 128
Taylor, K., 86
Thomson, N.I., 208-10
Times, The, 13-14, 17
Titmus, F.J., 122, 165-6, 175-6, 196, 199-200
Trent Bridge, 55, 85, 87, 131, 160, 165-6, 196, 198
Tyson, F.H., 42-3, 45, 49, 74-7, 82

Umrigar, P.R., 14, 86, 88, 90-1, 93-94, 211

Valentine, A.L., 52

Waite, J.H.B., 130, 133-4
Walker, P.M., 130, 132
Wallis Mathias, 160
Wardle, J.H., 31
Washbrook, C., 137
Watson, C., 108, 109, 110, 113
Watson, W., 31, 33, 75, 82
Welington, 180
Wesley, C., 132
West Indies, 10, 20, 22, 31-41, 44, 50-60, 67, 70, 83, 92, 106-124, 130, 136, 138, 146, 158, 160, 169, 187-8, 190, 216-18
Wisden, (Cricketer's Almanack), 22, 39, 152, 184, 201
Wooley, F.E., 89
Worrell, F.M.M., 55-6, 109, 114, 183-5, 191